Addiction

Matt Bell

© **Copyright 2024 - All rights reserved.**

The content contained within this book may not be reproduced, duplicated or transmitted without direct written permission from the author or the publisher.

Under no circumstances will any blame or legal responsibility be held against the publisher, or author, for any damages, reparation, or monetary loss due to the information contained within this book, either directly or indirectly.

Legal Notice:

This book is copyright-protected. It is only for personal use. You cannot amend, distribute, sell, use, quote or paraphrase any part, or the content within this book, without the consent of the author or publisher.

Disclaimer Notice:

Please note the information contained within this document is for educational and entertainment purposes only. All effort has been executed to present accurate, up-to-date, reliable, complete information. No warranties of any kind are declared or implied. Readers acknowledge that the author is not engaged in the rendering of legal, financial, medical or professional advice. The content within this book has been derived from various sources. Please consult a licensed professional before attempting any techniques outlined in this book.

By reading this document, the reader agrees that under no circumstances is the author responsible for any losses, direct or indirect, that are incurred as a result of the use of the information contained within this document, including, but not limited to, errors, omissions, or inaccuracies.

Table of Contents

Dedications And Shoutouts

Introduction

Chapter 1: Superman Died In High School

Chapter 2: Matt Is Fine

Chapter 3: School And Scouts

Chapter 4: My First Date With Oxy

Chapter 5: A River In Egypt

Chapter 6: The Day I Fell In Love

Chapter 7: The Time I Robbed The Scariest Woman I've Ever Met

Chapter 8: Less Than Zero

Chapter 9: "Treatment"

Chapter 10: Junk For Junk

Chapter 11: Selling What Other People Have

Chapter 12: Detox

Chapter 13: Retox

Chapter 14: Faith

Chapter 15: I Met A Girl, Then My Son

Chapter 16: Everything I Wanted

Chapter 17: I Go White-Collar

Chapter 18: Jail

Chapter 19: I'm Not An Alcoholic

Chapter 20: The Worst Date Ever

Chapter 21: The Two Worst Things I Ever Did

Chapter 22: Monica Is Kind Of Crazy

Chapter 23: Mom Does The Right Thing

Chapter 24: People Who Died

Chapter 25: The Card

Chapter 26: The 2015 Class Reunion

Chapter 27: This Time, I Listen

Chapter 28: Give It Away

Chapter 29: In Court, This Time By Choice

Chapter 30: Meet The Boss

Chapter 31: Don't Celebrate In The First Half (It's Always The First Half)

Chapter 32: Don't Think You Got This

Chapter 33: The Devil Never Goes Away

Chapter 34: How?

Chapter 35: Step 9

Chapter 36: The Guy In The Stands

Epilogue

Dedications And Shoutouts

This book is for my wife, **Monica**, the best woman that I will ever know. Every day I try to be a better man than I was the day before. I am who I am today, because of you.

This book is for my son, **Jackson**. If you're reading this right now, you're going to learn a lot about your dad. I hope this book inspires you and that you'll learn from my mistakes and my victories. You make me so proud to be your father. I love you, champ.

This book is for my stepdaughter, **Gigi**. You're the sweetest soul that I've ever known. I will always treat you and love you like my daughter. You are destined to be great! I'm honored to be in your life, and I'll make sure that I'm here as long as I possibly can be.

This book is for my daughter, **Giuliana**. Before I even met you, you completely changed the way that I view my life and the world. I will always protect you, provide for you, love you, and be there for you. You have changed who I am.

This book is for **my mom**. You never gave up on me. You always did what you thought was right by me. You didn't want to believe the worst about me. I will forever be grateful for you.

This book is for **Pat and Anne**, my in-laws. I love and admire you guys more than you know. You are such a huge source of inspiration. You've always motivated me to be a better person for

Monica. I've never wanted to call another man "Pops" after my father died… but Pat, you're "Pops" to me.

This book is for my friends **Kabir and Mike**. Two guys who have been consistent and loyal for as long as we've known each other. I never really knew what true friendship was until I met you. I trust both of you with everything and I wouldn't be who I am today without you.

This book is for **Dad**, the best man I've ever known. Every day I try to be a man he would be proud to call his son. I miss you so much.

This book is for everyone who gave me more chances than I deserved.

This book is for all the people who believed in me when I gave them every reason not to.

This book is also for those of you who didn't believe in me, or still don't. Read it and weep.

Introduction

Hi, my name is Matt. I'm an alcoholic and an addict.

You wouldn't know that by looking at me.

If you saw me walking down the street, you'd see a guy in a nice suit. You would see a guy who eats right and gets exercise, who keeps his hair well-trimmed. You'd see a guy who looks happy. You'd probably think that this is a guy who's got it figured out. You'd see a guy you can trust.

There's a lot you wouldn't see.

You wouldn't see the tattoos under my suit. You wouldn't see the dental bills of a man who'd been homeless for almost a decade. You wouldn't see track marks from using the same dull needle for months at a time. You wouldn't see the scars from scratching myself raw and bloody. You wouldn't see my criminal record. You wouldn't see that 10 years earlier, there was an illegal pistol in my waistband.

Everybody is two people. There's you on your best day, and you on your worst day. Most people never meet either of them. Few people are ever put into situations where they are tested so profoundly between evil or heroism. I have. Between the two, evil is usually the easier choice.

A person isn't the worst thing they ever did, and they aren't the best thing they ever did. I know who I am when I'm the worst version of myself. I've had to meet the most selfish, cruel, and depraved man that I can be. That's a man that I could be again in a heartbeat if I don't stay vigilant every second of every day. That man is still with me. But he's weaker every day.

I'm still working to find the best version of myself. Every day I'm closer. I hope to meet that man soon.

Call me a junkie. I don't care. Call me a dope fiend, a fuckup, a crackhead. That's fine by me.

A lot of people are offended by those words. I'm not.

I used to be an active, using addict. You call that whatever you want. It doesn't bother me what you call me.

In AA meetings, people introduce themselves like:

> *Hi, my name is Matt. I'm an alcoholic.*

I've seen people in AA meetings describe themselves as "a person in long-term recovery." Or they say, "I'm not an alcoholic anymore." They say, "That's not who I am."

Yes it is.

I am always going to be an alcoholic. For the rest of my life, I will be a junkie, dope fiend, crackhead. I'm just not actively using *right now*.

There's a movement towards being more sensitive about language, concern that labels will contribute to stigma. Multisyllabic euphemisms like *a person in long-term recovery* softens the blow. It hides the reality of addiction. It creates a separation between who you are today, and who you were the first day you came to AA and introduced yourself. Those aren't separate people.

Me today and me on Day One of recovery are the same. I don't care if you're sober for a week or a decade. Me and every other addict are just one bad decision away from going right back to where we were. The guy in the suit with the nice car—the respectable member of the community, the family man—is just one mistake away from being back on the street, hustling scrap metal and conning people for dope money.

When I say, *Hi, my name is Matt. I'm an alcoholic*, it isn't just to get to know the people in a circle at a meeting. It's for me. It's a confession, a reminder, and a mantra. *Matt, you are an alcoholic. Don't you ever think you can go back and get away with it.*

***

I've told the short version of my story many times. It's a big part of what I do. But this is the first time I've gone into my story in this much depth. Part of recovery is self-reflection. I'll be reflecting as I type these words, and you'll be here with me while I do it. Even the people who know me well haven't heard a lot of this stuff.

I'm keeping it as real as I can in this book. Expect a lot of foul language and foul behavior. I promise that my next book won't be as raw as this one.

I've changed or excluded some people's names. This is to guard them from more attention and scrutiny than they'd like. They didn't ask me to make them famous, and I'd like to respect that. It's also to protect me and my family, since there are some people mentioned in this book who might still be out there and holding a grudge. I'm not trying to get anyone in trouble. I just want you to know what happened.

***

One last thing. I'm not making a penny off of this book. Everything is going to research and charity.

I've seen other people sell their stories and make good money from it. I'm not speaking bad about them, but something about it doesn't sit right with me personally. As a parent, I want to share my knowledge and wisdom with my kids. I want them to know what they can do right—and what they should avoid—to have a good life. I want to spare them and I want to spare others. If my experiences can help others avoid that life, or help them escape it, then it was all worth it.

This isn't just my story. There are still a lot of people out there doing what I did and worse. There are people living on the streets. People destroying their bodies. There are children sitting at home, not knowing where their parents are. Parents and brothers and sisters who are afraid to answer a phone call from a number they don't recognize because this time the call could be *the one*. This could be the call from the police. The *last* call from the police.

I won't promise you that things will get better, or that it will happen soon. I've done enough lying for several lifetimes and I'm done with that, so believe me when I tell you that there is hope. If there is only one thing you remember after reading this book, I want that message to be it.

I am about to tell you just how bad it can get, but I'm also going to tell you just how good it can get.

Chapter 1: Superman Died In High School

Superman died in 1993. I was about six years old. Of course, Superman didn't stay dead. The writers of the comic followed up with a storyline where Superman came back.

My Superman died in 2001 when I was 14 years old. My Superman was my dad. There weren't any comic book writers to write a story and bring him back.

My dad was my hero. He still is.

I was blessed with a father who taught me morals. He taught me the value of hard work. He showed me what a good father was, so I could be a good father for my kids. He showed me baseball.

I love baseball. I love it. I've played the game my whole life. I remember one time back in 4th grade when I won the game for us by crushing a home run and making a diving play at shortstop. It was an incredible feeling. My dad was so happy for me. When I got home, I crashed on the couch for a few hours, and when I woke up, my mom was making dinner. The first thing I did was start telling her about the game, how well I did, and how I wanted to play baseball forever. Something about that caught my dad's attention; a blip on his dad-radar. He came to the couch where I was laying and took a knee so we would be eye-to-eye. He took my hands into his. Whatever he was about to say was going to be important.

"Son, I'm so happy for you and I believe you can be whatever you want to be. I know you love baseball. You're the best on your team, I think you know that. You should pursue it as long as you can… but please… never give up on school. I would rather see you walk across a college stage at the top of your class than to see you play baseball and be a star athlete. No matter what, promise me you'll never give up on your education. You're strong, but your brain is your most powerful muscle."

Parents pass wisdom to kids before the kids are ready to understand it. Sometimes it's years later that it finally makes sense.

Dad had a long view of things. Maybe he knew that too much fame and attention wouldn't be good for me. Maybe he knew me well enough—even when I was 10 years old—that if I made it to college ball, or even the pros, a lot of things can go wrong. Dad was always thinking long-term. He understood that pro careers might only last 10 years. He knew that an injury, politics, or just plain bad luck could end a career instantly. He knew how many athletes mismanaged their money and were penniless within a few years. Dad understood that an education lasts a lifetime.

***

After my parents split, we were asked who we wanted to stay with: Mom or Dad. It's a tough thing to ask a kid. It's hard not to feel like you have to choose favorites. My sister went with Mom. I went with Dad.

Most of the time, it was just me and Dad, and I really got to see who he was. Everywhere we went, someone knew him. We couldn't go to the grocery store without someone stopping us to say, "Hey, Roy!" It seemed like everybody knew him and everybody loved him. A hometown celebrity.

My dad was a man who always had to be doing something. Even after he retired, he needed something to do with his time, so he got a job as a mail carrier. When he wasn't at work, we went fishing or played baseball. I got that from my dad. It's hard for me to just do nothing.

Then one day he had some back pain and he went to see the doctor. The doctor figured it must be his job. Those mailbags can get pretty heavy. But the pain was getting worse. Finally, six months after his first visit, the doctors ran some tests.

Prostate cancer.

My father served in Vietnam. He didn't know it, but decades after he left that country he was still taking friendly fire. He'd been exposed to a chemical herbicide called Agent Orange. The US military sprayed it all over the jungles in Vietnam so that enemy soldiers couldn't hide in the trees. They didn't know it then, but Agent Orange also kills people. It just takes a really long time. America dropped about 20 million gallons of experimental chemicals from helicopters during that war. It's funny to think that nowadays, people are afraid to even throw a couple AA batteries in the trash.

There's no way he could have known it at the time, but my dad sustained a mortal injury the day he was exposed to Agent Orange.

Dad told me everything was going to be fine. I could tell he wanted to cry, but he held back. He spoke to me in his matter-of-fact way, "They are going to move me to another place and I'll get better there." They moved him, but it wasn't to another hospital. It was Hospice. He wasn't going to get better. It wasn't going to be fine.

I think he just didn't want me to be sad. There was no way to avoid that. Maybe he just wanted our final moments together to be as happy as they could be under the circumstances.

He didn't go through chemo or radiation treatment. He was well past all that. The cancer was already in his blood, bones, and brain. All they could do was to try and make him as comfortable as possible.

There's no story about a long, brave battle with cancer here. It felt like it came as quick as a car crash.

I remember visiting him in the hospital on Father's Day. It was a moment I would have liked for him to take my hand and tell me that I would make it without him. I wanted him to tell me to look after my mom and sister. I wanted him to remind me of the lessons he taught me, to tell me he was proud of me and that I needed to keep making him proud, even after he was gone. My dad didn't do those things, though. He asked me who I was and what I was doing in his room.

"What do you mean, Dad? It's Matt. Your son." I thought maybe his eyesight was gone.

No. The cancer was already in his brain. My dad looked at me like a stranger.

That fucked me up. That *really* fucked me up.

Just a few hours later, he died. Superman was real, but he wasn't ever coming back.

***

I didn't handle it the best way.

There's a creepy moment after a funeral where you have to return to normal life, but everything is just humming along like normal. People fill their cars at gas stations. People eat their omelets at a diner. People walk their dogs. Strangers go on acting like today is just any other day, like today isn't the worst day ever. People go on living their lives like the greatest man I knew wasn't gone.

So that's what I did, too.

A lot of kids might become reclusive and distant, or start acting out. I did the opposite. I continued on like everything was fine, and I sold it with a smile. Everyone checks in on you, especially when you are a kid—Mom, teachers, coaches, friends of your parents. No one knows what to say, because there isn't anything right to say. "How are you holding up? I'm sorry for your loss.

Your dad was such a good guy. If you need anything, anything at all…"

Matt is fine. "I appreciate your kind words, but I'm okay, really."

I still needed to get good grades. I still needed to make the team. I needed to fit in. I needed to just keep going. *Don't stop. Don't take time to reflect. Just keep going.*

The person most likely to believe your lies is yourself. I didn't know it at the time, but running away from this pain—pretending it wasn't there, even to myself, burying it under goals and activities—was the start of a bad habit. Ignoring pain was easier than feeling it. With practice, I got good at it, too. After a while, people stopped asking me how I was doing. *Matt is fine.*

Pain exists for a reason. Pain is there to tell you not to walk on a sprained ankle until you are healed. An injury doesn't heal while you're "walking it off." The same rule applies to the mind and spirit.

I was bullshitting myself about the pain I was in and I was good at convincing everyone else, too. As long as a kid gets good grades and does well at sports and keeps up appearances, no one thinks to ask if anything is wrong.

When a kid blends in, does what they're supposed to—especially if they do it in a varsity jacket—they can get away with almost anything.

That includes robbing drug dealers.

Chapter 2: Matt Is Fine

My sister was more of the rebel. She was the punk rock girl. I was always the good kid. I was such a straight arrow, I broke it off with my girlfriend in middle school because she smoked a cigarette and I didn't want to be around "that kind of person."

After dad died, I started to hang out with the kids who smoked cigarettes. I started smoking, too. They smoked more than just tobacco. I started smoking that stuff, too. They drank. I started drinking, too. Other than that, I did what I was supposed to be doing. I wasn't the guy that teachers keep an eye on. I wasn't the guy who other parents worry is a bad influence. Matt must be fine because he looks like he's doing fine. That's how it is. As long as a car's engine is purring, no one checks under the hood.

I played Baseball, Football, and Basketball. I'm like my dad that way. I can't sit still. Whatever I'm doing, I always throw myself into it. If I were studying, I'd obsessively memorize every vocabulary word. I couldn't sleep until I had mastered the material. If I was dozing off and had to sleep, I'd get up extra early to get back to it. Always 110%. I was like that with everything, including drinking.

It wasn't long before I was drinking about four days a week through high school. I smoked a *lot* of weed. I got high almost every day. I smoked before school, at lunch, and after school… and somehow I kept up my performance. I still got all A's. I excelled at sports. *See? Matt is fine.*

I'll never forget one game we played against Southview. I was a junior. I hit a home run, made an awesome diving play at shortstop, hit a triple off the fence (that was inches short of being a second home run), and closed the game pitching. There are those moments where you seem to consistently nail it; a perfect sports game, a party where every joke you tell lands, a job interview where you can tell every answer you give is just what they are looking for. This was one of those moments. And I was *so* fucking high.

When I was a kid, the DARE program warned us that marijuana was much stronger than it was when our parents were kids. These days, marijuana is insanely strong compared to what was around when I was a kid. Strains like "white widow" were rare to come by and scary strong. Me and the kids I was hanging with mostly smoked schwag weed, what people in Ohio called "mids." Before that baseball game, we got some crazy shit called "Blueberry Yum-yum." It had visible crystals and purple hairs. If it has a name, you *know* it's gas.

I had never been so fucking high before and somehow, I had the best game of my life.

It was soon after that game that I got this idea in my head that substances were enhancements. They made you better. They gave you more. They multiplied what you already had. Before a football game, we'd chug energy drinks and take these pills called yellowjackets that you could buy at a gas station or corner store. You can't find those anymore. They contained pseudoephedrine, which is a very strong stimulant. As it turns out, pseudoephedrine can also be used to make methamphetamine, which is why you can't buy it at gas stations anymore.

It wasn't just sports. I thought drugs and alcohol made fun more fun, they made you more likable, and made you a better dancer. The first dance I ever went to, I was a freshman, and I was drunk as hell from four Natty Lights. I walked in there with a swagger I'd never had before. In my mind, I had James Bond-level charm. That's why they call it liquid courage. I got a bunch of phone numbers and kissed a few girls. The lesson I learned that night was that beer was cool. Beer made me cool. Beer made me charming. Beer was fun.

I don't know how I didn't get caught. I was able to function. I managed it. I had it under control. I still did what I was supposed to do.

But actually, I didn't.

I got my driver's license on my 16th birthday. Later that day, I got a happy birthday DUI from the Rossford police department. I was loaded. Not just that, I had pills with someone else's name on the bottle and an ounce of weed on me.

It all got dismissed. I kept my driver's license. They didn't even give me points. I had some privileges suspended, but I could still drive to school, practice, and home. Those were the only places I went to anyway.

That wasn't the only time.

More than once, cops showed up at parties, responding to noise complaints. They recognized me and a couple other kids from the football team. They didn't call our parents and they wouldn't arrest us the weekend before a game. Maybe I started to feel invulnerable. I just kept pushing it.

I did worse than party.

I heard a tip that some guy in Genoa had a weed-growing operation on a farm, way out in the country. It would be easy to just walk in and take it, right? I recruited a couple solid guys on my football team and we planned it out during practice.

We drove out there at night, parked about three miles away, and walked two hours through the fields. Eventually, we found the barn. We crept in. It was empty, but we could smell the weed. It was strong. At least we knew the tip was good, even if the weed had been moved already. We looked around but there was nothing there. We almost gave up, but then someone lifted a large sheet of particle board. Bingo. There was a huge, underground storage with grocery bags full of cut, trimmed, processed weed, already divided into individual o-bags.[1] I have never before or since seen so much weed in my life.

There was so much, we couldn't even take all of it. There we were, three young, athletic, strong guys, and there was so much weed, we couldn't possibly carry it three miles in the dark. We took whatever we could, looping five bags on each arm. We could have planned this better. We weren't criminal masterminds, but we hadn't expected to find a haul that big, either.

We had more weed than we knew what to do with. We smoked it. We sold it. We gave it away to friends. I was selling it for about $100 an ounce. I could have charged a lot more. But while I had the stash, I was *the man*. I was the guy who had gas weed at mid-weed prices. You make a lot of friends fast like that.

One of those guys didn't do so well after the heist. That much weed wasn't good for him. He started getting bad grades. He started slacking at sports. He became a pothead. He went through a pretty dark phase, but I hear he's doing well now. For me, though? There were never any consequences. My grades were fine. My health was fine. And any legal problems I made for myself were excused, often by people who should have been trying to steer me right. I could tell myself I wasn't like him. I had it under control.

There could have been consequences. There *should* have been.

A varsity jacket and a 4.0 GPA were the perfect camouflage. If a pothead looks like a pothead—with greasy long hair, baggy pants, and a hemp necklace—they would get scrutiny from their teachers, their parents, their friends' parents, from cops. Even

---

[1] "O-bag" means a 1 ounce bag

something as simple as posture could be a subtle giveaway. But if you dress right, stand up straight, smile, and get things done, no one sees it, even when it's right in front of their eyes. When the kid who looks like a pothead has sleepy, red eyes, everyone assumed he was high. When I had sleepy red eyes, they thought I must have been up late studying. If you took that varsity jacket off me, though, me and the pothead were the same.

I kept getting away with it. Over and over and over again. I was getting high at games, getting drunk at school functions, getting busted (then released) by the sports fans in the local police department. When I was that age, if someone didn't stop me, I'd just keep going. Always pushing. Pushing, pushing, pushing.

There was a point I stopped. My girlfriend asked me to. She could see I was overdoing it. It wasn't causing problems between us, but she understood it wasn't good for me. So I did it. I just stopped. I gave myself 30 days, marijuana free, just to prove that I could. For the first few days, it was tough, but it got easier.

Those 30 days were good, too. Taking a break, I realized how much time I was wasting on it. You go get the weed, hang with the dealer for a minute, pretend to be friends, and sit on his couch while he plays Tony Hawk Pro Skater on his PlayStation. Then you go somewhere with your friends, find a private place to smoke. Then you go out and get some food because you got the munchies. Before you know it, you've lost about three hours. Instead of doing all that after school, I went to my girlfriend's house and had sober quality time together. It was nice.

When I was sober, I got home earlier. I got better sleep. I was better at sports. I should have seen right then the problem with my theory that drugs are an enhancement. And even though it was a good month, I was still counting down those 30 days. I wasn't sober because it was good for me. I was doing it because someone challenged me to do it. I needed to prove to them and myself that 30 days was no sweat. I dare anyone to tell me what I can't do. I love challenges. They are what make me move.

But the whole time, in the back of my mind, I was counting down those thirty days like a little kid counting down from December 1st to the 25th.

***

My dad grew up poor in Georgia. Dad was the youngest of 16 kids and he took care of his siblings. You didn't read that wrong. My dad, the *youngest*, took care of everybody else. My dad was built differently. Coming up that way, he learned to be good with money. He had to be. He was frugal. He wasn't cheap, but he knew the value of a dollar. When he moved up north, he wanted to give his kids a more comfortable life than he had.

That's why he gave me $130,000.

I inherited it on my 18th birthday, halfway through my senior year. That's a lot of money even in today's world, but in 2005, $130,000 was *a lot of money*. And most of all, that is a crazy amount of money for a kid in high school.

When I got it, I understood that this was serious. This was for real. This was the sum of everything my dad saved up. This was my future. I was going to college. I knew I needed to slow it down. But…

…for the next few months, *we are going to party.*

I moved out of my mom's house. I rented an apartment, and my place became the party house. I was one of the cool kids before. Now I was the fucking man. No curfews. Daily keggers. It was insane. It was stupid. It was not normal for high school kids to have this.

It wasn't the potheads and burnouts at these parties. It was "the good kids." The athletes. The cheerleaders. And I footed the bill for *all of it*. And with my dad's money, it wasn't hard.

My dad gave me that money because he trusted me with it. Maybe it wasn't a great idea to give that much money to a young man who doesn't know any better, but that mistake isn't on my dad. It's on me.

Have you ever wondered how rockstars can burn through their fortune in just a couple years? I don't. I know exactly how. Parties. Cars. Clothes. Trips. I'd burned through *half* of it before starting college. That's right. I blew about 70 grand just on parties. I was just giving shit away. I like doing that. I like to give to people. And it's really easy to be generous when you have more money than sense.

I graduated from my college prep school, St. Francis, with a 4.0 GPA, no criminal record, and a great athletic record. See? Matt is fine.

Chapter 3: School And Scouts

After high school, I had a full-ride to the University of Toledo; half athletic scholarship, half academic. I had offers from other schools, but I wanted to stay in Toledo. I wanted to be close to my mom. It's crazy thinking back on it. I turned down other opportunities to go all over the country. St. Francis is a good school and they are proud to say that 100% of graduates get college placement. Kids who graduated from St. Francis had options. Many went to The Ohio State University and The University of Michigan. Many went out to Chicago, New York, and California. Out of 200 or so graduating students, I was one of only maybe 15 who stayed in Toledo.

Maybe it was about control. Maybe it was about staying where I was comfortable, where things were familiar and I knew how things worked. Maybe it was because I was afraid of losing my mom like I lost my dad. Whatever it was, Toledo was home.

I did well at UT. I hit the books and I took studying very seriously. I was shredded and in the best shape of my life. I got great sleep. I showed up to practice early and left late. I was a Division I NCAA college athlete and I was going to school for free! And I had about half of that $130,000. Life was good. It was really fucking good.

For the first six months of my freshman year, I did exactly what I promised myself I would do. I slowed it down. I focused on school and sports. I was nailing it. I was living my dream. Hell, I was living a lot of other people's dreams. I had the world in my hands. Some people have so much and don't appreciate it, they don't even notice what they have. I did. I understood how lucky I was.

***

For a college athlete, scout day is a big deal. Scouts from all over the country visit schools to watch players and see who they think is pro ball material. For this exhibition, they split our team up into the blue and yellow teams. UT Baseball vs UT Baseball.

The pressure is indescribable.

I've played sports my whole life. I'm pretty used to people watching me and judging me. But it's a strange thing when complete strangers come from all over to watch you play ball for a few hours, to judge you, and to potentially choose the rest of your future based on how well you do. It doesn't matter if you got a bad night's sleep. It doesn't matter if your girl dumped you that morning for your best friend. All that matters is what you show them that day. No redos. No mulligans. That day was the day that would determine if my picture would be on a baseball card in some kid's collection some day. Either I was going to have my dream career, or I was going to have to settle for the second best thing, whatever that was. Just typing this I can feel my blood pressure going up.

I was the leadoff batter for the Yellow Team and I just so happened to be facing our team's best pitcher. Great. This guy was a *killer*. He's the kind of dude where you say, "Glad you're on my team!" This time, he wasn't on my team. This is how bad dreams start.

The first pitch was a fastball, low and in.

In sports, there are certain moments. Any athlete will understand exactly what I mean. Moments where the ball leaves your hand, or when you feel the crack of the bat, and you already know. You *know* you nailed it. Just the feeling of it. You don't even need to look and see. You felt it. The perfect crack on the bat where you know the ball is going exactly where you want it to. The spiral football arced for an effortless delivery into the arms of your tight end, so perfect that if it were an egg it wouldn't break. The feeling of the dimpled bumpy rubber basketball on the very tips of your fingers during a free throw, moments before that satisfying swish. It's a certain feeling, and if you haven't experienced it, I hope someday you do, because there is nothing else like it. It is a perfect moment, and it's not even a second long.

I hit a home run off the first pitch from our ace. You've never seen a bigger smile on my face. I *knew* the scouts noticed that one.

I played shortstop in high school. In college they had me playing mostly shortstop and a little bit of second base. It was the bottom of the inning. The batter hit a grounder between first and me at second. I went deep into the hole to field the ground ball. I get low, and let it bounce right into my glove, like how a puppy runs to you when you walk in the door. Then I turned that puppy into a double play.

They saw me crush a homer. They knew I could do that. I had to show them what else I could do. My next at-bat, I did the opposite. I laid down a perfect drag bunt down the third base line. That's the poker game of baseball. I love that mental part of the game. It's not just about swinging, throwing, and running. It's psychological warfare. It's the game within the game.

On my third at-bat, I hit a triple off the right-center wall.

The scouts got to see me hit a homer on my first swing. They saw me turn a double-play. They saw my offense and my defense. I got to show my arm. And with that bunt, I got to show off my speed. Scouts come with a list of things to score you on: athleticism, power, speed, knowledge of the game, and hand-eye-coordination. They got to see me kill it in every one of those categories.

Everyone has good days and bad days. You don't get a lot of truly great days. That day was the greatest day, the day I needed it the most.

I was versatile. I could hit. Centerfield. Short. Closing pitcher. Cleanup or lead-off batter. I could hit for power or I could hit to advance runners. I could be a pull-hitter or I could hit opposite field. I was a Swiss army knife. I could fit onto any roster. Everything went perfectly for me to show off everything I had. I could not have asked for a better game.

After the game, I talked to The Baltimore Orioles, The Oakland A's, and the Toronto Blue Jays. They liked me. They were scribbling notes about me. I was on their radar and I was still just a freshman. They told me to keep doing what I was doing and that they looked forward to seeing me next year.

After that game, I was like, "Holy shit. This is really going to happen. I'm actually going to go pro."

How could life possibly get better?

A couple weeks later, I got hurt.

Chapter 4: My First Date With Oxy

Many addiction stories start around 2006-2007. People old enough to remember will understand why. '07 was just before the peak of the opioid epidemic that affected every corner of America.

There's the part of the opioid epidemic that everyone already knows about. We all know how Big Pharma made stacks of cash on extremely addictive pills. Just last year, Purdue Pharma paid out $6B to settle a lawsuit for OxyContin.[2]

There's another part that fewer people know. A pharmaceutical corporation can make as many pills as they like, but they can't just put them on a shelf at Costco and sell them. Pharmaceutical companies can sell only as much as doctors prescribe. Just like cops, lawyers, and road construction contractors, doctors have rules. A lot of rules.

In '06, one of those rules was about measuring pain.

If you go to a doctor with an injury, they'll always ask, "On a scale from 1-10, how badly does it hurt?" They want to get a read on how bad your injury is, where the injury is, and what you need to manage the pain. If you say your pain is a 4, they'll tell you to take a Tylenol. Back then, if you said your pain was an 8, they'd give you something heavy, like OxyContin. If you are hurt so badly that you're screaming and can't even say a number, they might give you the really heavy stuff, like morphine and fentanyl.

In '06, the American Medical Association's (AMA) policy on pain was that only the sufferer could judge their own suffering. If

---

[2] Don't forget about this, because we'll come back to it by the end.

someone said their pain was an 8, as far as the doctor was concerned, it's an 8. The doctor had to accept the patient's personal diagnosis and prescribe the approved remedy. The remedy was almost always the same: opiates.

That meant that when a patient came in seeking pain management, a doctor couldn't just tell them, "No." There was hardly any oversight. Pain management clinics popped up overnight in exactly the places you'd expect: poor and desperate neighborhoods, the places where you can expect to find plenty of addicts. These alleged pain clinics were lovingly nicknamed, "pill mills," because they made their cash by handing out prescriptions and collecting insurance payments. Essentially, these were drug dispensaries, paid for with public dollars for the profit of private investors.

You may have noticed that the word "opiate" sounds a lot like opium. That's not a coincidence. Opium is the dried latex from the opium poppy plant. Opium is used to make heroin. The truth is, there isn't much difference between the pills your doctor prescribes for a sprained ankle and the stuff you buy from a sketchy dude in a trap house, besides reliable dosage and quality for the prescribed stuff.

But it gets worse. In '08, the real estate market tanked. You don't need a big economics lesson here to understand it. It's enough for you to know one key fact: the average middle-class American has most of their wealth invested in their homes. The crash knocked 30% off that value in a flash. America hit a major recession overnight. The economy was riding high for a decade on easy credit and bad investments. The party was over. In '08, the hangover began. People watched local businesses go under, dropping dead like mayflies. Buildings and houses went empty and stayed empty. Americans watched their towns slowly disintegrate. I definitely saw it in my hometown of Toledo. There was a dramatic spike in unemployment. A spike in divorce. A spike in suicide. There was a spike in every indicator that our society was unwell. And one of those indicators was a rapid increase in addiction.

The market failure created all the social and economic conditions that lead to addiction, and at the exact same time, opiates were easier to get than ever. But, wait. There's more.

Something else was happening at this time, but it's less well-known. Afghanistan was run by Islamic fundamentalists called The Taliban until 2001, when the United States invaded in the earliest moves of the Global War on Terror. The invasion had an unexpected consequence that hit America at home, and it had nothing to do with terrorism. The Taliban, being very religious and anti-drug, had outlawed farming poppies. Remember that poppies are used to produce heroin. With the Taliban gone, the extremely poor farmers of Afghanistan were again able to produce a very profitable plant. By 2007, Afghanistan was producing 93% of all heroin in the world while the United States military was occupying it. Oops.

Easy pills. Economic collapse. New drug production abroad. A supervillain in a volcano lair couldn't plan a more perfect situation to start an opioid crisis.

There is the stereotypical addict. The ghetto welfare queen. The trailer park trash. It's easier for people to turn up their noses at addiction if they can mentally push them all into a category of people they look down on. It's easier for people to wrap their heads around it when they can just dismiss addicts as bad people. The crack epidemic of the 1980s hit hard, but it stayed in certain neighborhoods. Most Americans could think of it as someone else's problem. Not so with the opioid epidemic.

People you would never suspect started getting hooked. People would see a doctor for ordinary ailments—broken bones, arthritis, and sprains—and go home with a prescription for high volumes of extremely addictive drugs.

Your dear aunt Linda who had surgery for breast cancer—a woman who goes to church every Sunday and keeps Precious Moments figurines on her mantle—became addicted to a heroin-analog. Your cousin Steve broke his wrist and lost his basketball scholarship, and came back home with no plan for his life except a bottle of pills for his wrist. Your best friend's dad got a repetitive motion injury in his hip from working his butt off at the Jeep plant for 25 years. He got some high-octane pills and a little time at home to recover, but was laid off before he returned, and the man never recovered. Your high school buddy who came back from fighting in Afghanistan with a metal leg and chronic pain, both physical and psychological.

This wasn't just hitting the people who society can ignore. This was coming home. When the people closest to you get hooked, it's harder to believe that addiction is something that happens to bad people somewhere else.

Legendary talk radio conservative Rush Limbaugh became addicted to opiates after a back injury. According to his arrest warrant, in August of 2003, Limbaugh purchased about 2,000 pills of Hydrocodone, Lorcet, and Norco over six months.[3] That is a *lot* of pills. Limbaugh had his staff running around full-time getting him hooked up. He needed those pills just to get out of bed and do his job every day. Most people don't have a staff. Most people aren't famous. Most people don't have millions of dollars to spend. Most people's jobs are tougher than sitting and talking for a few hours a day. Imagine what a regular person has to do to feed an addiction?

While doctors were handing out pills like Halloween candy, people who didn't get hooked could make fast cash selling their leftovers for as much as $50 a pop. With easy money like that, it's

---

[3]https://www.washingtonpost.com/wp-dyn/content/article/2006/04/28/AR2006042801692.html

no surprise that there were so many patients whose pain never seemed to go away. There was a surplus of pills, a growing market of addicts, and new opportunities for entrepreneurial street dealers.

This story isn't just important because it created so many addicts. This epidemic put regular people face-to-face with addiction in a way that many had only seen in movies and in the news. Good people were getting addicted to "hillbilly heroin." People you knew and loved. The old lie that drugs were just a bad moral choice made by bad people couldn't hold up to scrutiny.

And when the policy for pain management changed and doctors became much more cautious, the addictions didn't just go away. When doctors got out of the dealer game, Afghani poppy farmers were there to take over the supply side.

If you were hoping there was some silver lining to all this, there it is. People get it now more than they ever did before. Addiction affects so many lives, and most of them are the friends and families of addicts. This is the story of millions of Americans. It's also my story. I was one of these people. I trusted a doctor when I thought he was prescribing me medicine. Like many people, my story starts with an ordinary injury.

***

I hurt my shoulder turning a double play in practice. I went to the doctor and got an MRI. Torn rotator cuff. It was a two-hour outpatient surgery. It went well, they told me. I wasn't worried. I'll still be able to play my four years after I recover.

The doctor sent me home from the hospital with a bottle of 90 30mg Percocets and 5 refills, a total of 13,500 milligrams.

In '06, that sort of thing was common. Like everywhere else in the country, Toledo was in the middle of the opioid crisis. They gave me all those pills for *outpatient* surgery.

I got back home, and was hanging out with my roommate, watching TV, and it was time to take my first pill. One every four hours, or whatever it said on the label. About 15 minutes later, I got up to go to the bathroom. That's when it hit. Maybe the blood flow from standing up triggered it.

As I was stepping into the bathroom, I remember this intense feeling all over my body. This stuff was hitting me like no other substance ever had. Beer and weed didn't come close. This was an almost orgasmic wave that washed over me. I held onto the towel rack to brace myself, wondering if this was just a head rush that would go away. It didn't go away. What is this? I've never felt anything like this. How would I even describe it? Almost… cozy. This must be what it feels like to be cuddled by God.

I remember saying out loud, "Holy fuck. I want to feel this way every day. For the rest of my life." I heard myself actually say those words, and it didn't sound insane to me.

Chapter 5: A River In Egypt

I can get obsessed. I can get obsessed with work. I can get obsessed with a sport. I can get obsessed with anything that I enjoy. That's a good thing when it's pointed at things like career and family. It's a double-edged sword, though, because that same energy can be pointed in the wrong direction.

I instantly became obsessed with Percocet. Before I was out of that bathroom, holding onto the towel rack, I was obsessed.

My thinking at the time was simple math: if one beer is good, five is better. If one Percocet made me feel this way, what would two do? Or three? Or four? Those 90 pills were supposed to last me a month. They were gone in a week. I ate these things like they were M&Ms.

Two of the side effects of opiates are nausea and itching. I experienced both. I threw up and scratched myself like I'd rolled in poison ivy. And I loved it. Not at first. But after a while, I even began to love the itch. I threw up a lot and I learned to appreciate something so disgusting because if I had my face in a toilet bowl, it meant I was high.

I needed to maintain. I still had school. I still had practice.

Another side-effect is poor sleep, *especially* when you stop taking them. I woke up one morning and I was freezing cold. My bones hurt. I felt nauseous (but not the good kind when I was high). I couldn't even look at food. Terrible diarrhea. Cramps. I thought I had some super flu. I had no idea that this is what withdrawal feels like. I had only been taking the pills for seven days.

I googled the symptoms on my Compaq laptop. Every hit on the first page said the same thing. *Addiction. Dependency. Heroin addiction. Withdrawal. Addiction.* Nah. That can't be right. So I went to page 2. Same thing. Page 3. Page 4. How often do you go past page 1 of Google? I went down to page 10. Every link said it. *Addiction*. I didn't want to see it. I slapped the laptop shut.

> *This isn't me, man. I'm not an addict. I've got 70 grand in the bank. I'm a Division I college athlete on the shortlist for three MLB teams' potential drafts. I have my own place. I have a girlfriend. I have a Motorola Razor flip phone. I'm not that guy.*[4]

Ten pages of Google search results didn't convince me. Maybe I got a bad pill. Maybe it's just a Percocet hangover or something.

***

What An Addict Looks Like

> Everyone has their own idea of what a full-blown addict looks like. They aren't hard to spot. These new opioid addicts weren't like them. They weren't chap-lipped and scratching themselves and trying to sell you a hubcap. The new crop of addicts didn't even understand they were addicted. They got up and went to work and did regular stuff. They didn't have to do scary drug-addict stuff. They didn't have to drive into the most dangerous part of town and do a hand-to-hand through a car window, while three guys with Glocks in their waistbands watched from a porch. No, they could use the much less dangerous CVS drive-thru to pick up their dope. They didn't have to go into a busted-up drug den, and step over and around a half dozen addicts nodding off, to go meet some guy named "Tank." No, you made an appointment with a doctor's office.

---

[4] For younger readers: believe it or not, having a Motorola flip phone was impressive in 2006.

They weren't living like "junkies." They didn't have to see scary drug-addict stuff. Not yet. They could still say to themselves, "I'm not an addict. I'm taking medicine."

That was me. I was that guy. For a long time, I was that guy. I was that guy long before I even tried Percocet. I just didn't know it yet.

***

It's hard to get reliable information about these things, but it was *so much* harder back then. If you wanted to know about drugs, you had to know someone who did a lot of them. I called up a friend, a party guy who knew this stuff better than I did. I told him my situation.

"I think you might be addicted," he said.

"No. You think? No way."

"Here's what you do. Go get another pill and take it. If you feel better, that's your answer. Maybe it means you're addicted."

His idea made sense to me. It was almost scientific. And best of all, it meant that I got to eat another pill. But I was out of pills and couldn't get a refill yet. I had to find a dealer. My friend knew about pills and coke and all the other stuff that I'd never tried. He got me in contact with a guy. I went and got another pill. I took it. The symptoms vanished right away. I was fine. I wasn't even high. I was just normal.

I didn't know how addiction worked. I thought you had to be a user for years to become addicted. What I didn't understand was that I was hooked the moment that first pill hit me.

"Oh my God. I'm addicted to these things." I couldn't keep bullshitting myself. Before I even had a moment to process this, the next thought interrupted. "Shit. I gotta be in class in 10 minutes."

Chapter 6: The Day I Fell In Love

Most people can take a Percocet and stop. Some people can't. I can't. And there's only one way to learn if you're like most people, or if you're like me and millions of other addicts. You take the drug. You either become addicted, or you don't. The only way to know is the worst way to find out, like looking for landmines in a field by walking right into it.

Denial is one of those words that's become its own cliché. Things become cliché when they're overused and predictable, because they're so common, because they're so expected. But that's why clichés are often real. Denial is real. After withdrawal, I was faced with the fact that I was one of them. One of those people they warned me about in D.A.R.E. I was the person they warned elementary school kids to stay away from. I was the person I was told not to be around.

Nope. That's not me. I'm not that. No fucking way. The addicts I read about in school had trench coats and lurked in alleys. That's not me. Addicts hang out on street corners and beg for change. I'm an A student. I'm an elite athlete. I'm not wrong. 10 pages of Google results are wrong. *Matt is fine.*

Denial doesn't have a long shelf life. Reality will always impose itself. There's a moment when every addict realizes they are hooked. That moment is the same for everyone, no matter what the addiction is. It's always the first time they can't have the thing they are addicted to. That feeling knowing that life is about to be very uncomfortable. The feeling that your brain's neurochemistry has taken on a lot of debt and the collector is knocking on your door.

The problem I faced was like locking your keys inside your car. The problem and the solution are the same thing. I still needed to go to class. I still needed to get to practice. If I stopped taking those pills, I'd be too sick to do either. I needed to take a pill at night to sleep. I needed to take a pill when I wake up so I could get to practice. I wasn't anywhere close to confronting the psychological part of addiction. I was simply managing the physical dependency. But managing dependency was the part I liked.

It's addict mentality. An addict can always think of seemingly logical reasons to do drugs. Whatever the question is, it always has the same answer: take the drugs. I needed to test myself to see if I was addicted. Take drugs. I need to get to sleep. Take drugs. I need to get to school. Take drugs. Not taking drugs would mean I can't get all these things done. Not taking drugs means I can't get to practice. Not taking drugs means I won't play for Baltimore in two years. In fact, it would be irresponsible of me to not take the drugs.

What was the question? Who cares? The answer is always *take drugs*. It's easy to con yourself into believing the answer is drugs. The self-deception is bottomless. That's addict logic.

***

I went to class. I went to practice. I did what I was supposed to. That's what I told myself. I kept buying percs, dipping into that 70k. Then the 70k was 68k. Then 65k. It goes quickly and the more you have, the quicker it goes. Every day I was at the ATM pulling cash and watching that balance wither away. I didn't just eat the percs anymore. I was crushing them up and snorting them, bypassing the whole digestive system, right to the mucus membrane, which is just around the corner from the bloodstream. Snorting eliminated any timed release in a pill so it hit faster and harder.

I should have called my doctor. They would have told me to stop taking the pills. They probably would have referred me to a clinic to detox. Instead, I was taking addiction advice from the best expert I knew: a dealer/user.

Then one day my dealer didn't have percs. Her source dried up. Maybe the source got busted. Or maybe my dealer just had a new plug, because now she was selling Oxycontin. OC-80's packed a lot more punch and went for about $70 a pill. I started my oxy career with just one a day. What's $70 when you have 130,000… no, 70,000… no, wait, $55,000 in the bank?

My rationalization, my self-bullshitting told me that I needed the opiates to get through the things I needed to do. That didn't last. I was getting terrible sleep. My performance on the field was declining. I was losing muscle mass faster than an astronaut. I started skipping classes and showing up late to practice. Doing well and acting like everything was cool was my camouflage, but it was wearing off. People were going to notice. Maybe they already did.

***

NCAA did regular drug tests every week. Usually, it was only two people, chosen randomly. Every week I played Russian roulette with my scholarship and ball career. Every week, the tester would call the names, and every week two guys who had nothing to worry about pissed into a little cup. It was only a matter of time before they drew my number.

It's not like they were gunning for me. It was random. And they knew something was wrong. I'm sure they'd seen it plenty of times before. I had insurance through the university. If I had just gone to them they would have helped. But I loved opiates so much. That's something sober people don't understand. You think I should hate the drugs because of what they're doing to me. At the time, I didn't hate drugs. I *worshiped* them.

***

Most of my time was spent getting high as fuck. People tend to hang with people who share their interests. My #1 hobby, my #1 priority, my #1 aspiration was getting high. With an attitude like that, you don't have much to talk about with sober people. That's why I started hanging out with other people who snorted oxy like I did.

By this time, about a dozen of my close buddies from high school were all using, taking oxy every day. A few of them got onto it the same way I did, but most of them started recreationally. Someone offered it to them and they tried it. A lot of times that someone was me. A couple paragraphs ago, I said I loved getting high. I worshiped it and I wanted to share it with others. It was like missionary work. I was here to spread the good word. I shared with them the oxy gospel. One of the sickest things about a drug habit is that you *want* other people to share it with you, like knocking on doors and asking people if they've heard the good news.

Everyone I shared it with loved it. New converts are always the most zealous believers. We pooled money to buy in bulk for a discount. We helped each other doctor shop. We were more like fellow cultists than friends.

The money started running thin. I was doing 4 or 5 pills a day. That's $400 every damn day. I was putting more money up my nose in an afternoon than many people my age made in a week. I was snorting enough to pay rent. The thing about unlimited money is that it always runs out faster than you think it will.

I needed to make that money last. Snorting it made it stronger, more high for less money. Someone had the cool idea to try shooting it. That hits harder, right? I guess. None of us had ever shot up anything before. It sounded right. But how?

YouTube is pretty amazing. You can find videos of anything. You can find videos of people building log cabins. You can find hundreds of hours of videos of sea turtles. You can find a tutorial on how to change the oil on a 2003 Honda Civic. You can find a tutorial on how to do Hollywood movie-quality special effects makeup. You can also find video instructions on how to shoot oxycontin. And that's what we did. We watched some guy on YouTube.

Crush the pill into a fine powder. Cook it with some water in a spoon with a bic lighter until it dissolves like sugar. Break off a filter from a cigarette, and use that to filter the drugs as you suck it up into the syringe. Tie off your arm with a makeshift tourniquet. Stab. Inject. Release tourniquet.

We all shot up together, at the same time. We didn't know if it was safe. We were all new to this. That's how strong our devotion to opiates was: it was damn near a suicide pact.

We survived. It worked. It was stronger. Damn. It was so much stronger. I laid back and vanished into that calm swimmy feeling and floated off. None of us ever went back to snorting.

***

I loved the needle. I don't just mean pills. I mean the needle itself. I got weird with it. I loved experimenting with it, injecting into different veins, just to see what the difference was. It didn't just stop with drugs. I shot up Jack Daniels one time and got insanely drunk in a few seconds. It was extremely dangerous. If I didn't have a pill, I'd shoot up water, just because I loved the ritual. People have nervous habits like biting their nails or pulling their hair. When I was stressed, I could calm myself down by shooting anything, it didn't even matter if it got me high.

I was clean and meticulous. I only used purified drinking water. No one else was allowed to use my needle water. I always had alcohol swabs to clean the injection site, just like a nurse would do at a hospital. That was how I started, anyway. I won't be so picky later in the story.

Chapter 7: The Time I Robbed The Scariest Woman I've Ever Met

I knew a dealer, let's call her Latifa. She lived in a pretty rough area near Detroit and Bancroft. If you are from Toledo, you know exactly what I'm talking about. If you aren't from Toledo, let me put it this way. The police department installed "shot-spotters" in that neighborhood, which automatically detect and triangulate the source of gunshots.[5] Half the houses in the neighborhood were boarded up, abandoned, or condemned, the paint peeling, the wood swollen from rain and humidity. Black mold splotches on the limp, hanging wallpaper inside. But Latifas's house was nice. Easily the nicest house on the block.

Latifa was a tall black lady with gold teeth. You couldn't step into her house without being thoroughly sniffed by her two huge, poorly-trained pit bulls. When I said her place was nice, I mean *really* nice. She had marble floors and red suede curtains. She had a huge high-end fish tank, but instead of exotic tropical fish, it had ordinary goldfish in it. Her place was halfway between how a young rapper who just made their first million would decorate their home and Buckingham Palace.

Her boyfriend was huge. Scary huge. Absolutely-not-to-be-fucked-with huge. He had jheri curled hair and was always wearing a wife-beater. Gold chain and gold teeth. If you've ever seen the TV show Snowfall, he's the uncle in real life.[6]

---

[5] Shot-spotters are devices that measure the volume and sound of loud cracks. They can tell the difference between gunshots and firecrackers and can triangulate the source of the shot. As soon as a gun pops, the police know exactly where it popped, even before anyone calls the police.

[6] *Snowfall* is a great show about the crack epidemic in South Central LA in the 90s. If you haven't watched it, you're missing out.

I never saw that woman without a lit blunt in her hand. "Whassup, Matt," she'd say, always stretching out the vowels like, "Whaaaassuuuuup Maaaaatt."

She loved me. Every time I came by, I was there to give her money. My friends and I brought her thousands of dollars of business a day. I brought her new customers. Of course she loved me.

She was nice because she *could* be nice. She didn't *have* to act tough. Everyone understood that she was not fucking around. Everyone knew not to give her a reason to stop being nice. So she got to be nice. That made her terrifying.

We never came through the front. She always wanted us to come through the back alley. I gave her a phone call to let her know when I was there. "Okay, I'll be right out." I waited by the fence and a gate. But instead of just coming straight to the gate to meet up, she always detoured through the detached garage behind her house, in through the access door, and then out through the big garage door. It didn't make sense.

That's how I knew she kept her stash in there.

I could call her anytime. I didn't need to tell her I was on my way or give a head's up. I could always call from the alley right when I arrived.

"Whassup Matt?"

"Hey, I'm here."

"I'm sorry, I'm in the bath right now and I don't have anyone here who can meet you. Just take a drive around the block, get a bite to eat or something, I'll be out in 10 minutes."

"Okay."

I hopped her fence, and slipped into her garage. It was empty. Totally bare, not even a toolbox or a bottle of motor oil. There was a pile of dirty clothes in the corner, with a spare tire on it. I moved the tire and dug around through the clothes and found a small, Louis Vuitton bag. Cha-ching. The garage was "empty" just like that barn full of gas weed in high school.

I found three full baggies of oxys, one with 20s, one with 40s, and one with 80s. About 500 oxys total. I didn't even need to steal it. I had the money. I was planning on buying them until she told me about the bath. I didn't need to rob a dope dealer. I *definitely* didn't need to rob a dope dealer who would kill me and feed me to her pit bulls. But I was down to 15 grand in the bank and it felt like I was quickly running out of road.

I grabbed her shit, hopped over the fence, threw it in my car, and circled the block. I got a call. "Hey, Matt. I'll be out in a second."

"Okay."

I parked and walked back to the gate. She came out and did her usual detour through the garage, but this time it took a little longer for her to come out of the garage.

She called me back.

"I'm sorry, Matt. I don't know. I guess I must've misplaced it. I'll have to look around."

I said, "Okay, well… call me as soon as you find it. I'm really sick. Please." And the Academy Award for best actor goes to Matt Bell. If I'd been cool about her not having pills, she would've known that I robbed her. And I kept going there every single day, like usual, and I always bought at least one pill. If I stopped coming to her after she lost her whole stash, she'd know who robbed her.

I told her I was cutting down. I started buying my normal five pills, then the next week just four, one fewer every time. I had 500 or so of her pills, but I had to keep coming and buying them to keep up appearances.

Finally, I told her "I think I might quit altogether. I might go to rehab or something like that, so you might not see me around like you're used to." And then I lived off her stash for a while.

It wasn't just a mistake to rob a very dangerous woman. It was a mistake to let myself have that many pills all at once. I only bought a few at a time. I never bought the whole pharmacy. It was an all-you-can-shoot buffet.

For the next two months, I was blackout high. I mean that. I barely remember a thing.

Chapter 8: Less Than Zero

I told my coach the biggest, most unbelievable lie I could ever tell.

"I don't love baseball anymore."

The truth is, I couldn't stay and wait for the NCAA drug test to finally find me. The stress of getting caught was constant and unbearable.

He didn't buy it. He already knew what was up. I thought I was good at hiding it, but I was constantly late, nodding out at practice, and 20 pounds lighter than when I joined the team. He didn't call me a liar, even though he knew I was.

He just said, "Matt… if there's something going on… if something's wrong… please. Let us help you. We have resources. We don't want you to get in trouble. If you're going through something, please, just tell us. We can help you."

He knew. I knew he knew. He knew I knew he knew. But I lied anyway. I played it like he was worrying for nothing. *Matt is fine.*

"Oh, no, it's nothing like that." I said it like he was being ridiculous. "No, it's not anything like that. I appreciate it. I just don't love baseball anymore. I'm going to go work at Jimmy Johns."

I don't know why I even said that. There's no way he'd believe that I'd rather make Turkey Toms than play in the MLB.

I didn't have the courage to talk to my teammates about it. I quietly emptied my locker when no one was around. I simply slipped away. No goodbyes. I vanished like a ghost. And just like that, my athletic scholarship ended. I became financially responsible for the semester. That wouldn't work, because my budget was earmarked for dope. I couldn't pay for the last semester, and I couldn't enroll for the next.

There was no way to hide that I wasn't in school anymore, that I wasn't on the team anymore. So I lied. I told everyone that my shoulder never really healed properly and the team couldn't commit to keeping me on. It's a classic story that everyone already knows: a promising young man's bright future was destroyed with a career-ending injury. It's a cliché, which made it easier for other people to believe my bullshit. I made myself out to be the victim of a freak accident.

I did end up working at Jimmy John's for a little while, getting as high as I could as often as I could. A full-time job at Jimmy John's does not pay well enough to support a full-time drug habit.

Then I ran out of money.

Seeing my bank account hit zero was the worst feeling. It wasn't just money. Zero wasn't just a number. That money meant something. That was the money my father spent his life working so hard for. No one knew he had that kind of money because he didn't live big. He wasn't showy. He drove a 20-year-old car. He lived with less so that I could have more. That money represented his love for me. That money was his hope that I would have a good life. He gave me a chance that very few people get. He gave it to me and not my sister because I was supposed to be the responsible one. I was the one who would make the most of it, invest it, nurture it, and make it grow. And once I was doing well, then I could help my sister and mom.

It wasn't really my money. It was my family's money. I was just the custodian.

And I blew it all.

At this point in the book, you might be thinking I'm a real piece of shit. I don't blame you. That's exactly how I felt about myself, too. That last dollar was the last thing I had that connected me with him.

***

When you're broke and addicted, you get creative and morally flexible. I was fired from Jimmy John's for stealing. I was changing the tip amounts on credit card receipts. A $5.00 tip was transformed into a $15 tip just by adding one pen stroke. A simple little scam that lasts right up until someone actually checks their credit card bill.

I had no money. No job. I lost my apartment. I moved back in with my mom.

The law finally caught on to what was going on. Those pill mills were getting popped and shut down. It turns out that it was just three doctors in Southeast Michigan and Northwest Ohio that had been feeding the entire city. The day the police raided those clinics was a bad day for three doctors and about 50,000 addicts.

The pill supply dried up quickly. Dealers couldn't get the pharmaceutical grade opiates anymore. Zero supply, and a ton of demand. It was the perfect market for the cartels to jump into.

I called my new dealer constantly asking if more pills had come in yet. His phone must have been ringing non-stop, because I know I wasn't the only one calling.

Finally he called me back. He didn't have any pills, but he offered me an alternative. "I got a new plug with some new stuff. We're gonna try this out. It's cheaper. It's stronger. It lasts longer. First one is on the house. I'm just giving out samples."

"I'm on my way." I didn't even ask what it was.

It was black tar heroin. I shot that up right there. For only $20, I was high all day. It had a gentler comedown. I woke up the next day thinking, "That was good. That was so good."

It's not hard to see why heroin hit Toledo—and the rest of America—very hard, very fast. Doctors gave people addictive drugs. The law took them away just as quickly but they didn't take away the addiction.

I started with percs in '06. Six months later I'd graduated to oxys. A year and a half after that, I was mainlining heroin. That was the same year I got arrested for the first time.[7]

***

There's a "food" in Haiti called bonbon tè. It has three ingredients: salt, fat, and dirt. They look like cookies. They don't eat these because they love the taste. Rich people don't eat mud cookies. Eating bonbon tè is the kind of thing that people do when they need to trick their body into thinking they've eaten real food, just to temporarily stop the hunger pains.

Addiction reminds me of that. It's like hunger. When you're starving, hunger overrides everything else. Oxy always took priority. Food? Who cares? Sleep? I don't need it. Sex? Waste of time. When you are dope sick, every other item on Maslow's hierarchy of needs gets wiped off. It's just a triangle with only three letters on it: oxy.

My unlimited money ran out just like that. Everyone's heard stories about people who won the lottery and are broke a few years later. That's me. I won the lottery. I was broke two years later. It scared me shitless how fast that money went. It scared me to think what things were going to be like when that balance was below zero and over drafted.

Like with those Haitian mud cookies, when you are starving and don't have money, you'll do things you'd never do with a full belly. If you ever want to make yourself upset, take a minute to read about the famine in Ukraine in 1938. A starving person will

---

[7] We'll come back to that story in a couple chapters...

eat anything. If it gets bad enough, they'll eat tree bark, shoes, and other people.

That's what we did.[8]

No money means no dope. No dope means you feel and behave like your survival depends on getting more dope.

We got selfish. The worshipers who learned how to shoot dope on YouTube, we all turned on each other. It got ugly. There are a lot of thieves in the world, but only an addict will steal from a friend and help them look for it.

"You're missing a pill? Did you check the couch cushions?"

An hour later, after exhausting every other possible place it could be, we unscrewed a floor vent, just in case it fell down there. Meanwhile, it's in my pocket. I was stealing from the same people that I had invited into this addiction. I didn't feel like I could be gracious with them anymore. I remember when it was easy to be generous my senior year in high school, when I had a full bank account and more weed than I could possibly smoke. That was all over now.

That guy with the trench coat in the alley—the one they warned me about in D.A.R.E.—I was becoming more and more like him every day. I loved sharing and giving to these people a year earlier, and now I was taking from them instead. Selfishness takes over. An addict only has friends for as long as they have dope.

---

[8] Not literally, of course.

Chapter 9: "Treatment"

My mom figured out that I was an addict. She didn't want to see it for a long time, but eventually, there was no way to deny it. The act was over. No one could believe Matt was fine anymore.

She let me stay with her on the condition that I went to get treatment. I agreed. The first time I went to treatment was at a methadone clinic.

Methadone is controversial. It was invented by German scientists during WWII for pain management. Methadone isn't known for that, though. It's mostly known for addiction management. Methadone clinics were the medical system's first attempt to answer opiate addiction. These places are basically small clinics that only do one thing: distribute the opioid methadone to addicts.

In some clinics, you come in and talk to security first and you give them your number, not your name. You take a seat on a plastic and metal stackable chair in a waiting room full of the people staying at the homeless shelter across the street. You wait a while. Eventually, they call you up to a window with bulletproof glass, like a gas station in the hood. You show them your ID to confirm your identity. They check your file and give you a tiny plastic cup with some bitter red liquid in it. They watch as you drink it right there. Then you say, "Thanks, see you tomorrow," and go on with your day.

It rides the line of "First, do no harm." Like I said, they're controversial.

The clinics look harmless enough, but believe me when I say that they can lock down faster than a maxi cellblock when they need to. They deal with addicts all day every day, which means they constantly deal with desperate people who lie and steal.

Methadone clinics come from a philosophy of harm reduction. It's a very practical perspective. When people get methadone from a licensed clinic, they know they won't get a bad batch or a dangerously high dose. Generally speaking, nurses are safer than drug dealers. Since there are no needles being passed between strangers, there's less risk of transmitting blood-borne illnesses such as HIV and hepatitis C. Patients can get what they need and get on with their day. I won't criticize anyone who uses these clinics if it really helps them stay off the needle, if that's how they can get a job, if that's how they can get their kids back. When clinics are doing that kind of thing, I believe they are a net positive. At the very least they're keeping these people alive one more day. Who am I to judge?

However...

Methadone is a huge revenue stream. And they are still giving addictive opioids to people. The patients of these clinics are still hooked on a drug. They may be better off than they were, but as long as they keep getting their doses, they won't be able to fully heal. Let me be clear: I mean heal *literally*, not just in the psychological therapy sense of the word.

One of the side effects of PEDs (performance-enhancing drugs) like steroids is that they will shrink your testicles. That's legit; it's not an urban legend. The reason is simple: testicles produce testosterone. It's not a coincidence they share the same first four letters. Steroids *are* testo. That's why another side-effect is acne. Juicing is like starting a second puberty. When a man takes super-human doses of testosterone, the shots are outcompeting his balls. His balls become obsolete. When the body has more T than it knows what to do with, the huevos go into hibernation. You can file this fact under "Things I didn't want to know about Mark McGwire."

Opiates do the same thing to the brain. Opiates don't mess with testosterone, they mess with the brain's ability to produce dopamine. Dopamine controls a person's ability to feel pleasure and joy. It is the center of the brain's motivational system: If you do something good, you feel happy. If you do something bad, you feel bad.

If you take drugs for years and years, the same thing that happens to an athlete's balls will happen to your hypothalamus: it becomes obsolete. It goes into hibernation. Your body can no longer create dopamine normally. You physically *cannot* be happy from anything *except* drugs.

There are only two ways out: get sober and suffer the years necessary to heal the damage, or take more drugs. People usually take the second option.

An injured rotator cuff won't heal if you keep pitching. An injured body part needs a break. A brain injured with drugs won't produce dopamine correctly. As long as someone is still getting regular doses of methadone, it never will.

I wish methadone wasn't pushed on people seeking treatment so quickly as a first option. Some of these clinics aren't treating people, they're just stealing customers away from the cartels. It's mailbox money. It just comes to them. It's like a subscription model. It's free money, just like my old dealer Latifa, who spent all day hanging out in her beautiful home, waiting for money to come to her.

I don't want to smear all of these clinics. Many places really do care. They make sure their patients are hitting their benchmarks, that they're passing their drug tests, that they are getting the right dose, and making sure they are still seeing their therapist.

Other places don't give a single fuck. As long as medical billing processes them without a problem, they'll hand out drugs and send people on their merry way. I've seen clinics that let patients come in high. There are places that will still give methadone to people who fail their drug screen over, and over, and over again.

They'll give patients take-homes for the weekend, which the client turns around and sells them for money to buy heroin. The staff knows. They just don't care. You can tell the staff you'll do it, "Thanks for the methadone. I'm gonna sell this for heroin," and they won't do anything about it. They call it a non-punitive approach.

The first clinic I ever went to was that second kind, the don't-give-a-fuck kind. There were no methadone clinics near where we lived at the time. My clinic was in Monroe, Michigan, just on the other side of the border, about 25 minutes away. They only accepted cash because they wouldn't take insurance from out-of-state. Since I had a fake job that paid literally nothing, my mom footed the bill.

I remember walking past prostitutes soliciting in the clinic parking lot, next to cars with people slouching low so they could shoot up without being seen by a passerby.

I met a dealer at a clinic who became addicted to his own product. He got on methadone because he couldn't make money as long as he kept dipping into his own supply. This was the kind of dude who wore flashy gold everything because he wants you to know from a block away that he sells drugs. One time I watched him pull out a fat wad of cash and slip a few bills to a nurse through the small opening in the bulletproof glass for some extra take-homes. They didn't make an effort to hide it. It came so easily to both of them, that you'd think he was getting a pack of Kools from the carry-out.

***

I played the role of the recovering addict, but I wasn't recovering. I was going through the motions. I was playing my part. I was "getting my life back on track."

I had a job selling Kirby vacuums door-to-door. It's a perfect job for someone pretending to be in recovery. I worked alone. I didn't have a supervisor with me every day to notice if I wasn't doing a good job. I worked on commissions. I wasn't going to get fired for not selling vacuums fast enough. It's hard to sell a vacuum to anybody. Most people already have a vacuum. What are the odds that I knock on your door and it just happens to be the day your vacuum broke? And these things sold for like $1,500. It was ridiculous. I wasn't selling vacuums. I wasn't making money.

But I could say I have a "job." I was in "treatment." And that was the bare minimum I needed to do to keep my mom from riding my ass. I was still spending time with other addicts who were also pretending to be in recovery every single day.

Addiction is a full-time job, with no pay, no benefits, and the worst hours imaginable. Talking to another addict is almost like talking to a coworker, a colleague, which means you mostly talk to each other about work. That's how I learned about scrapping. That's how my victimless crime of drug abuse went to the next level.

Chapter 10: Junk For Junk

To this very day, I am banned from every single scrapyard in the state of Ohio. I'm blacklisted. There is a database all these places share to keep an eye out for people who do what I did.

Scrapping is a euphemism for stealing metal and selling it to scrap yards. As long as you don't get greedy, you can get away with this scam for a long time. Scrapping paid a lot better than vacuum sales, so scrapping became my job. It became my whole day. I looked for metal junk and sold it for money to buy the other kind of junk. Once in a while, it was legitimate metal junk left on the side of the road, like a busted washing machine on the curb. Most of the time I stole it.

I took Telegraph Road between my mom's house to the methadone clinic and back every day. My happy hunting grounds. Every day I'd look out the car window for things to steal. Car parts from a Jeep dealership. A tractor supply store. A mobile home park, where a kid carelessly left a scooter on the front lawn. Aluminum siding. A spindle of copper wire. A bicycle chained up next to a Subway. Even the chain and lock on the bicycle next to the Subway. When you start looking for metal, you'll see it everywhere.

What's the best place to steal junk? The one place that is nothing but junk. A junkyard. That was my thinking, anyway. What I didn't understand yet was that scrap yards are owned and operated by people who are always looking out for people doing exactly what I was doing. A scrapper stealing from a scrapyard is about as smart as a jewel thief stealing from a Sierra Leone diamond mine.

Stealing is easy. Getting away is when everything goes wrong. The first time I got caught I was robbing a yard in Michigan, just on the other side of the border.

I thought I was in the clear as I finished loading the scrap into the back of my truck. The guy spotted me and said, "Hey you!" It may as well have been a starter gun at a 100-yard dash. I hopped into the driver's seat of my truck and hit the gas and zipped out as fast as I could. As I turned onto Telegraph, I took a sharp turn. I heard the unmistakable scrape and clanging sounds of metal. In my rearview mirror, I watched everything I'd stolen spill out onto the road. I was in such a hurry, I forgot to close up the back latch.

Telegraph Road is mostly straight, and this stretch has two lanes with a median and a speed limit of 45. I was going nearly 100 mph because the guy from the scrapyard was in his truck and right behind me. He didn't stop to collect his stuff that I'd just spilled all over the road. He didn't want it. He wanted *me*. He was keeping up, driving just as fast as I was. I was strapped into 7,000 pounds of metal and plastic, going so fast that I was crossing the length of a football field every 2 seconds, weaving in and out of traffic faster than the speed of thought.

I passed a cop car. I knew I had just a few seconds before they were after me. I dumped my kit out the window: syringes, spoons, and any other paraphernalia I didn't want to be caught with. Just as soon as I'd removed any possibility of a drug charge, I saw the cherries and berries, the red and blue lights of a police car. Running from a junkyard was one thing. Running from the cops was smoke I did *not* want. I pulled over, like any good, responsible motorist. The guy chasing after me slowed down and pulled over, too. He got out and explained the situation to the police.

That was the first time I was arrested. First times have a way of sticking in your memory.

At the time, I thought it was bad luck when a cop spotted me going twice the legal speed limit. Thinking back on it now, it might have been good luck for me that the cop got to me before the dude chasing me did. Or worse. What if I hit something? What if I hit some*one*. I might have died or been paralyzed. I might be writing this story from a jail cell for aggravated vehicular homicide.

It's possible that the cop saved my life. If so, that'd be the first of two times.

I was still new to this. Back then, I didn't understand the criminal justice system. If I'd kept my mouth shut and lawyered up, I might have been able to beat the charge. I didn't exactly have the evidence on me, because it was all in the street a mile back. I confessed right away. Deep down inside, I was still a nice kid who didn't get in trouble. I cooperated with the police because that's what my parents and teachers taught me to do.

The police cuffed me and put me in the back of their car. It's one of those things that isn't quite like you expect. It isn't what you see in the movies. The seats are made out of hard plastic. There's a half-inch thick plate of plexiglass in between you and the police. There are no handles on the inside for me to get out. There are no seatbelts, which would be illegal if I weren't in a police car. The police weren't angry. They weren't even concerned. They were bored. It was like they worked at a grocery store and had their lunch break interrupted by the manager asking them to clean up a spill in aisle 5.

They took me to Monroe County jail. I sat in a cell for a few hours, alone with my thoughts and four walls of white-painted brick. Holding cells are like sensory deprivation chambers. There's no color. There's hardly any sound. You're surrounded by white nothing. Just a metal toilet with a drinking fountain on the back. Eventually, someone tells you you're just about to be released, they just need to process you. Then you don't see or hear from anyone for three more hours.

The police let me out that same day. They didn't even tow and impound the truck. They let me go with my wallet, phone, and keys, and I was able to hitch a ride back to my truck just a mile or two away, still at the scene of the arrest.

I went straight to the spot where the police spotted me because that's where I'd thrown my spoon and needles. Miraculously, they landed on the side of the road and were in perfect condition. Getting those back felt like finding your lost wedding ring before your wife noticed it was missing. Like Linus finding his blanket.

Then I went and got high.

***

After a few weeks, you develop an eye for scrapping. Most people look at a used car battery and see a used car battery. I saw a price tag. How much can I get for that? Who would buy it from me? What does it weigh and how difficult is it to transport? How much can I steal? What are the odds I don't get caught? I quickly and subconsciously did a math equation. Insurance companies have complex mathematics to figure out the risks and rewards of any policy and come up with a number. I subconsciously did the same thing, but the only three possible answers were:

1. Steal it.
2. Don't steal it. Look for something else to steal.
3. Fuck! I can't find something better to steal. I'll have to steal it.

It's amazing how much I had to learn about metal to be good at stealing it. I always had a magnet on my keychain. Aluminum, copper, titanium, stainless steel, whatever it is, if the magnet doesn't stick, it was worth top dollar. Like I said before, when I get into something, I go all the way.

When you're desperate, you get sloppy. I remember walking into a scrapyard with a brand-new, beautiful 10-foot aluminum ladder. I tried to play it as straight as possible, as though these people would be stupid enough to believe that I'd sell a perfectly good $500 ladder for $20.

Every scrapyard has to deal with this, which is why every scrapyard has a cop. It's that big of a problem, that police officers just hang out like a hunter in front of bait, waiting for someone to do the stupid thing. Scrappers know this and still they *always* take the bait. I did. Over and over again.

One time I snuck onto the construction site of the Skyway Bridge over the Maumee River on I-280 and stole a truckload of metal. This wasn't some rusty junk. This was pristine, high-end metal used for a suspension bridge. Of course, I didn't come into the scrapyard looking like a foreman on a city job, with a helmet and reflector vests. I looked exactly like what I was: an addict with $20,000 of metal in the back of a truck. I might as well have tried selling a pristine 1984 Ferrari Testarossa at a flea market.

Right away the cop asked, "Where'd you get it? If you work with us and tell us where you got it, maybe we won't charge you with a felony."

I have been arrested three times at every single scrapyard in the area. In some places, more like four or five times.

***

When I was a kid, people gave me a pass. Most of the people who would have enforced consequences were people who knew me, who wanted me to do well, and who cared about me: my mom, my coaches, and my teachers. As an adult, all that protection goes away. I had run out of passes. That shit stopped. After I turned 18, those consequences finally found me. Anytime after that, when I got caught, no one let me go with a warning. They put me in a cop car and took me to 1622 Spielbusch every single time. It might be a book and release, just an hour inconvenience. The system didn't care about me. It doesn't know me. It doesn't *even* hate me. That's why they call booking "processing." That's exactly what it is. A credit card company processes your request. A chicken nugget factory processes chicken. That's all it is. The system processes you, holds you, gives you a court date, and maybe releases you. Or they keep you.

I've been busted all over the country and no matter where I went, it always worked that way. Just like that methadone clinic, they dispassionately go through the steps, the process, the routine, and then they eject you onto the other side. You're another criminal passing through the criminal justice drive-thru, and the staff will forget you the moment you leave.

By the time I was living the consequences I'd been sheltered from as a teenager, it was already too late. I didn't give a shit about the consequences. I was way past that road marker because that's what addiction is: repeating behavior despite consequences. If drinking is destroying your marriage, a normal person will stop drinking. An addict won't. The addict is a polygamist with two spouses and doesn't want to divorce Jim Beam.

Getting arrested didn't stop me from scrapping. Scrapping was my go-to. As long as you only scrap actual junk, and you don't bring too much too often, a scrapyard will take what you bring them without too many questions.

But even better than stealing junk, is stealing *not* junk.

Chapter 11: Selling What Other People Have

Drug addiction isn't a hobby. It isn't even a job. It's a vocation. A career. A hobby is something you do when you have time. A job is something you put minimal effort into because you are there for the paycheck. A career is something you have to master. It's a set of skills that are rare and take a lot of time and real-life experience to acquire. A career is something you take with you when you go home. Addiction is a career. For me it felt like a calling. There are no days off. There are no vacations. You are always on the clock. You are always on call. It's always your shift. It's always overtime without pay. There are no bathroom breaks. You might think addiction is a job without a boss. That's not true. Not even close. You have a boss. He's the worst, most cruel boss you can imagine. And he's always there because he is in your head.

Addiction is like getting into debt with a mob boss. Anyone who's watched The Sopranos knows the rules: pay on time, or the difference is added to the principal. That's illegal, of course, but people don't borrow money from gangsters when they can borrow from a bank. The payments are so damn high it's impossible to catch up. With addiction, the gangster is your own brain's limbic system. You can't go into witness protection to hide from yourself.

When people are in debt to gangsters, they will do things they would never do otherwise. It's not just money. It's the fear of getting their kneecaps shattered with a Louisville slugger. It's the fear that someone will torch their home and take the insurance check. It's the fear for the safety of their family.

When you are in it with bad people, first, you work hard to get caught up. But you can't get caught up. You're not supposed to get caught up. The meanest kinds of gangsters don't want to settle up. They want a constant, reliable income stream. Working hard doesn't get you caught up, so you sell everything you have. That gets you through a short time, but the game is rigged. You can't work to catch up. You can't sell what you have, because it's already gone. So you sell what you don't have. You sell what other people have. That means stealing. That means embezzlement, insurance fraud, or some other form of larceny.

Toledo is like a lot of American cities. Some neighborhoods are beautiful, safe, pristine, a place where they don't hear gunshots and return fire at night. Then there are the opposite kinds of neighborhoods... the ones you wouldn't want your mother's car to break down in, only a half mile away, but just far enough away that the gunshots don't disturb the people in the nice neighborhood.

The nice neighborhoods don't have bars on their windows. They don't lock the car in their driveway. People keep some very expensive things inside their garages with the doors open all the time. These are places where they don't worry about security because they don't think they have to. They forget that they usually have better stuff to steal and they're not as far from crime as the home value rates want them to believe.

I'd put my bike into the back of my truck and drive out to a nice little Toledo suburb. I'd drive around until I saw something promising. I'd park three blocks away, take my bike out of the truck bed, and ride back to the house I'd already cased with a glance. I'm not a threat. I'm not an addict. I'm just like you, enjoying a bike ride.

I'd make sure the coast was clear, ride right into the garage, and grab a leaf blower. Or a power drill. Or a circular saw. Or even another bike. Maybe I'd get lucky and grab a Cannondale with a carbon-alloy frame. Every garage had something valuable in it that I could sell for at least $20. Whatever it was, I had a guy.

I knew a guy who would buy anything for lawn care: leaf blowers, snow blowers, weed whackers, and lawnmowers. I had a guy who would take bikes and do them just like a chop-shop, break them down for parts, and remove any evidence that would lead back to the poor guy who stepped out to take a ride one morning and asked, "Honey? Did you move my bike?" There were always buyers.

***

In the state of Michigan, going into an open garage that is attached to the home is considered a home invasion, which is a pretty serious charge. I learned that when I went into the attached garage of a police detective who was still at home. He came out just as I was leaving. He didn't hear me. It was just bad luck. You can make the right decisions all day, every day, but you can't always be lucky. He chased me down the block and got my license plate number as I got into my truck and drove away.

It wasn't hard to find me. That was the second time I was arrested.

Besides open garages, one of the next best places to steal from are the trucks of lawn companies. They usually park out front, take what they need as they need it, and do most of the work in the backyard. It's not too difficult to drive right up next to one of those trucks and help yourself to an edger or a backpack blower.

That's what I was doing the third time I was arrested.

As I'm writing this, I realize that the details of each arrest get slimmer. Each arrest feels less like a story and more like a regular part of my routine. Steal stuff. Usually get away with it. Sometimes I get caught. Try to run. Get busted. Get released. Repeat. And I didn't even care anymore. You get processed when you get arrested. But at this point, getting arrested was just another process in my life. It's just something that happens. Your job is to steal things, sell them, and buy drugs. The state, cops, and courts' job is to catch you, process you, and release you. It's nothing personal. It's just part of the routine.

***

A Good Kid From A Good Family

> I was a pretty good kid growing up. Before I discovered that I loved beer, I did what I was supposed to. Just like I was playing the role of son in recovery for my mom, I could play the role of "good kid who just got mixed up with drugs and the wrong crowd" for a judge. I'd tell the truth. I was a straight-A St. Francis kid from a good family. I was an athlete who had everything going for me until I had a sports injury and became addicted to Percocet. I would tell lies. "I'm in recovery. I'm trying to turn my life around." My backstory was worth a lot of goodwill with the judges.
>
> I'd do short time. 30 days here. 60 days there.
>
> Sometimes, instead of jail time, they'd sentence me to treatment. I'd go and do the things I was supposed to, talk to the clinicians, go to the meetings, and then as soon as I was home, I'd go back to using. Sometimes it *almost* worked. Sometimes I'd clean up, get out, and really want to stay sober. But I always thought I could do it halfway. I'd still want to go out and party. I still wanted to drink. I still wanted to hang out with my friends that still drank and smoked weed. In no time, I was back to using. It always took me back, eventually.

***

I stole and then I got caught or I got high. Every day. Lie to Mom. Every day. It was the routine. During this period of my life, things tend to blur. Just like you probably can't remember what you had for dinner two Sundays ago, I don't remember every arrest, every clinic, and every theft. I can't always remember the order things happened. Time kind of smears together, because everything I did was just like an ordinary day at the office.

One night, the cops saw me walking down a main street in east Toledo, carrying a saw and a bag of power tools at 3 in the morning.

They approached me and said, "Hey."

"Hey," I said back casually as if we were just strangers being polite as we passed each other on the sidewalk.

They didn't keep walking, though. They stopped me to ask a question they already knew the answer to. "What're you doing with a saw and power tools at 3 a.m.?"

"They're mine. I'm just taking them home." A big mistake right there. A person who hadn't stolen them wouldn't tell a cop "they're mine" if the cop hadn't asked who they belonged to.

It is very difficult to talk a cop out of doing their job. If they've been at the job for more than a year, they'll assume everyone is lying to them all the time. Usually, they're right. When they saw me walking, there wasn't a chance in hell they weren't going to ask for my name and ID, and run them into their computers. There wasn't a chance in hell they weren't going to see I had bench warrants for skipping court dates. There wasn't a chance in hell I was going to just say, "These tools are mine, officers. I'm a good citizen, walking home at 3 a.m.," and they would believe me. I lied anyway.

Even as they were arresting me, I was begging them, "Please, take care of my tools. Don't just leave them out here. I need them for work."

"They'll be safe in the evidence room."

I spent the night in jail. They let me out the next morning. I walked straight across the street and into the safety building where they were holding my tools[9] in evidence. I approached the clerk behind the desk and said, "I'm here to pick up my stuff."

If I didn't try to get the tools back, it would look more suspicious. The legitimate owner would ask for their tools back. Maybe I'd get lucky and they'd let me take them.

They ran my name. "Mmm yeah, no, you're not taking those power tools home."

Like Wayne Gretzky said, *You miss every shot you don't take.*

---

[9] Which weren't mine.

Chapter 12: Detox

What is your worst fear? Think about it for a moment. You'll know you have it when you don't want to think about it for even one more second. Your worst fear isn't spiders or heights or ghosts. Your worst fear is watching your parents grow old and infirm. Your greatest fear is failing to live up to others' expectations. Your greatest fear is becoming like your mother. Your greatest fear is that you waited too long to have kids and now you don't know if you ever will. Those are the things that are so scary, that you feel uncomfortable reading them right now.[10] A well-made drama should be more terrifying than a horror movie.

When you're addicted, your worst fear is withdrawal. You will do literally anything to avoid experiencing it.[11] Most people never have to face their worst fear. But I did. Over and over again, I lived my worst fear. I was in and out of rehab. I'd go because I was ordered by a court or to appease my mom. I might stay a little while, four or five days, but I'd usually leave AMA (against medical advice). Mostly, I had withdrawals because I was stuck in jail for the night. Every single time that happened, I had to face down the thing I spent all my time and money avoiding.

***

Imagine I've never tasted chocolate in my life. No brownies, no cookies, ice cream. Nothing. How would you explain chocolate to someone like that? It's sweet, but it's a little bitter... but those

---

[10] Or hearing them, if this is an audiobook.
[11] People overuse the word "literally," and insert it into sentences for emphasis. You could say, "Dave Chapelle was so funny, I literally died." Obviously, you did not *actually* die. It's kind of how people use the word "fuck" for emphasis. "Dave Chapelle was so funny, I fucking died." When I use the word literally here, I *literally* mean literally.

words aren't enough. Sweet like what, strawberries? No, not really. Bitter like aspirin? No... more like... bitter like coffee, but not exactly. But chocolate does go great with coffee... It's smooth... Like mashed potatoes? No, not like potatoes at all.

You can't really explain it to someone who hasn't had it.

And that's what drug withdrawal is like. It's impossible to describe perfectly because it's not like anything most people will ever have to experience. I'll do my best to explain it but understand that it's like me describing chocolate as strawberry-coffee-aspirin-mashed potatoes.

Imagine the worst flu you ever had. For most people, that would probably be Covid when it first hit. Multiply that by the worst hangover you've ever had, then multiply that by a number so high that you don't know the word for it. You ache like you died but you are still somehow conscious to experience your muscles go through rigor mortis. Joints hurt like advanced arthritis, the kind that makes your hand clench up like a bird claw. Your skin hurts. Your fucking *hair* hurts. It feels like there is something under your skin, crawling around, like a colony of centipedes are burrowing around. Some people scratch themselves until they are bloody to get at them, but hallucinations are hard to catch. Everything is too bright. Everything is too loud. You are shivering cold and scorching hot at the same time like someone is pressing dry ice on your peeling sunburn.

You feel like you're about to vomit, but there's nothing in you because you can't eat. You take a sip of water, and you throw it up immediately. Food looks disgusting, but you know you have to eat. You try and fail over and over. Even just chewing food sends shooting pains in your jaw, like the guy from those Saw movies was performing a dental exam. You will shit yourself until your body runs out of anything to shit, which doesn't take long because you can't eat. You can't sleep. Sleep would be a brief escape. There is no escape. You will feel every bit of this and nothing will take it away but the thing that got you here.

This isn't a 12-hour thing. This goes on for days, or weeks, depending on how serious your habit is. I didn't sleep for 23 days the last time I went through detox. I don't even know how I lived through that. My body would give out, shut down for maybe 11-minute stretches, then shake me awake again. If a person did to me what I did to myself, they'd be in violation of the Geneva Conventions. Nazi war criminals awaiting trial at Nuremberg were treated more kindly than what I did to myself.

That's just the physical part.

Emotionally, it is pure sadness. It is the deepest, most perfect sadness. It is the kind of sadness you feel a few times in your life when you experience the greatest tragedies.

For years, you've been artificially pumping feel-good chemicals into your body. For years, you doused your brain with unnatural levels of dopamine. So your body stopped making it on its own. Your brain's entire system for experiencing joy and happiness has been damaged to the point that it doesn't work anymore. You broke it. And it takes *years* to fully heal. Without that system functioning properly, we experience a world without happiness. It seems that the default setting on a human brain is the darkest, cruelest misery imaginable… but it's not imaginable. Not unless you've been there yourself. Hopeless to the point that you don't even have the energy to kill yourself.

For a solid month, it is physically impossible to feel good.

But I haven't even told you the worst part yet.

The worst part is knowing that this will continue for weeks. Your brain is running like a rat on a wheel, just thinking the same thought over and over and over again: *you can make all of this stop.* You can make it all vanish *right now*. You just need $5 and a phone call to your dealer. I can beg 20 people for a quarter and have $5 in an hour or two. Detoxing is the worst thing you'll ever feel, and turning it off is as easy as buying a can of Pepsi from a vending machine.

I didn't chase dope to feel good. I chased dope to hide from *that*. Every damn day that monster was close enough I could feel the wet heat of it breathing on me, nipping at my heels every second of every day, always just inches out of its grasp.

So yeah. That's kind of what detoxing is like. But it's worse.

***

I went through the hardest part of withdrawal in the worst place to experience it: inside a jail cell, twisted up in a blanket that was damp from my sweat, and trying not to make any noise that would wake up my celly. A month later, I still didn't feel right. Things didn't have the same color they used to. There was a fog in my mind.

That first treatment center I went to was one of the nicest. This wasn't a dumpy methadone clinic. This was a legitimate treatment center in Florida. It wasn't the kind that famous movie stars go to, but it was really nice. I was about 20 at the time. I stayed in a co-ed halfway house. Some of you might be thinking to yourselves, "Co-ed halfway house? That's a terrible idea!" For everyone else, keep reading to find out why they're exactly right. Even the rehab told me not to go to that one. But me being in my 20s, I wasn't quick to turn down the company of women.

Over the course of my drug-abuse career, I was in and out of rehab all the time. 30 days here, 30 days there by order of the court. I was forced into treatment, or I went to make my mom happy. I never really gave treatment a chance. Of course I didn't. I was *forced* to do it. It's like the saying goes: You can intubate a horse and force-feed it water, but you can't make him thirsty. That's not exactly the saying, but you get the idea.

The only time I went voluntarily was that first time. I was just… sad. I didn't want to be in trouble anymore. I didn't want to be doing it anymore. I wasn't insured at the time and it helped that those places sometimes give scholarships. I got in because someone vouched for me. It was the same story I kept hearing and kept telling over and over again: good kid, fell in with a bad crowd, struggling to get right…

***

While I was there, the staff said something to me I should have listened to right then. Maybe I did. I dismissed it right away, but for some reason, I remember it.

They said, "99% of people use drugs because something happened. 1% of people just really like drugs and alcohol too much."

I said, "I'm just that 1%. Nothing happened to me." *Matt is fine.*

The next thing I *wish* they'd said was, "99% of people say they're in that 1%."

I blew it off, but it stuck with me. I remembered it every time I was in treatment, because every psychiatrist, clinician, and therapist at every rehab I went to always asked me, "Was there anything traumatic in your past?"

And I always said, "No. The nicest treatment center I was at told me that I was in the 1% who really just love getting drunk and high." That was my own fictional retelling of what they *actually* said to me. I never worked on anything. I was just going along with it.

In group therapy, me and other recovering addicts would sit in a circle. People would unload. They would share the horrible things that happened to them and the horrible things they'd done to others. I related with them on some of it. But I still held on to the fantasy…

> *I'm not fucked up like these people are. I'm different. None of them were athletes. None of them are as smart as me.*

I was terminally unique. It was the exact same lie I told myself years ago when I first ran out of pills and started feeling sick. I'm not an addict. I'm not like those people. I'm going to play professional baseball. I was still doing it and I couldn't even see it.

Addicts lie. They lie all the time. They lie to doctors, they lie to their families, they lie to cops, they lie to judges, they lie to their friends. More than anyone else, addicts lie to themselves. An addict who can't stop lying will never get sober. My greatest fear wasn't withdrawal. I thought it was at the time, but that was another lie I told myself. Withdrawal was my *second* biggest fear. I was willing to face my withdrawal a hundred times if it meant I didn't have to deal with what I was really afraid of, what I'd always been running from.

This wasn't just about pills. The story of my addiction started before the first time I popped an oxy. I was ripping off drug dealers long before I discovered opiates.

I never would have pulled that shit while Superman was still alive. Never.

Hey, look at me. Do I look like I have a problem? I'm fine. Matt is always fine. Matt doesn't have a problem. Matt doesn't have *problems*. Matt doesn't have vulnerabilities. Sometimes dads die. No biggie. I'm fine. *Matt is fine.*

***

Rehab ended for me when I met a girl.

Her name was Dawn. We met. We used. We left treatment. We took off to her hometown of Pittsburgh and stayed with her folks. I repaid their generosity by stealing their jewelry. They called the cops and kicked us both out because they didn't know which one of us was responsible for the jewelry coming up missing.

All-in-all, my first rehab experience did not go very well.

In the movies and TV, states are always extraditing prisoners to face justice for their crimes. Unless it's murder or some major crime, it's not like that. Think of it from their perspective. Some addict thief fled the state, he isn't ever coming back, and we don't have to pay to try and incarcerate him. Sounds like a win. Good riddance. I went back to Ohio. I continued on as I always did.

After that, every time I was stopped by cops and they ran my information, they always let me know, "You have warrants in Allegheny County, PA. It's not extraditable, but just so you know." Whatever. PA doesn't want to come and get me, so I'm a free man.

Chapter 13: Retox

Days, weeks, months, years vanished into my arm just like my dad's money. One day, I realized that everyone I knew from college graduated and moved on. They don't even know me anymore. I wasn't part of that world anymore. I was fully a member of the Toledo active addict community. I didn't have teammates or coaches anymore. I didn't even really have friends anymore. I had accomplices.

When he was alive, everywhere my dad went, people knew him. Now I was like that, too, but with dope addicts and thieves.

I knew the main heroin plug in town. I could run errands for him for free dope. His place was set up. A house in the hood with Fort Knox security. The guy was always around and always had four or five cars parked in front of his house. It was wired up with surveillance, and this was back before everyone had those inexpensive Ring cameras. His windows were tinted like mirrors, so you could never see inside from the outside. He had a staff, maybe 30 guys working for him full-time. He was *the guy*.

His supplier was a Mexican cartel. All the heroin coming into Toledo came through him. Every other dealer in town was just a middleman.

One time, I was getting sick on a Saturday night. The guy wasn't home. I knew he would be at the bar partying, so I waited outside his house until 2AM for him to get home.

When his car finally pulled up, I approached him as he was getting out and I said, "Listen, man. I'm sorry to be outside your house like this, I know you don't like this, but I have money and I am so fucking sick right now..." I didn't need to tell him. He could tell I was in pain just looking at me.

He was drunk and was coming home from a good time. He was off his game and in a good mood. Instead of getting mad, he invited me in. "I want to show you something."

He took me inside his place and down into the basement. He had a trap door built into the wall. On the other side, he had guns. Lots of guns. Not quite that scene in The Matrix, but enough to make me realize he wasn't just your average dealer. And he had a huge safe. He opened it up to show me it was full of bricks of uncut, black tar heroin. I couldn't even guess how many millions of dollars worth. I knew he was the guy in Toledo, but I didn't understand that he was a serious heavy-hitter.

He knew I wasn't a threat to him. There was no way I could ever steal from him. He just wanted to show off a little bit. I have to be honest. I was a little scared. This guy was no joke. His operation had to be bigger than just Toledo.

Along with the bricks, there was a sandwich bag with heroin that had already been cut and stepped on and ready for sale. He sold me that bag.

Soon after that, he got popped. There was too much traffic outside his house. Too many people knew. The cops had been watching that house for years. The way it usually goes is when someone gets arrested, they rat on someone higher up for a lighter sentence, that person rats on someone, and on and on, until the police find whoever's at the top. With him gone, the entire heroin supply was gone, too.

***

Things were getting bad out there. People were selling fake heroin to desperate addicts. I remember one time I worked all day just to make 20 bucks to pay for some heroin from a dude who told me he had some plug up in Detroit. I took the bag without checking and rushed off to somewhere safe to shoot up. I opened the bag and tapped some powder into a spoon. As soon as I started cooking up with a Bic lighter, I could smell that I'd been ripped off.[12] It wasn't heroin. It was powdered hot cocoa. It was Nesquik.

I shot it up anyway.

I had to know for certain. I had to make sure it wasn't heroin that was cut with hot cocoa. I was so dope sick, I probably would have shot up anything you put in my hand. I didn't shoot it all at once, just a little bit, just to test it. It's amazing how much punishment a human body can take. I might be the first person to have ever experimented with mainlining hot chocolate, and to my surprise, nothing happened. I didn't even get a sugar high.

That was one of the times I went to rehab. It wasn't because I'd hit rock bottom. Even shooting Nesquik wasn't rock bottom. That wasn't even the last time I did something like that. You might remember a few chapters ago, when I was talking about first falling in love with the needle, that I always used purified water, and that I always sanitized my needle. That didn't last. Nine years later, I shot up using water from a dirty puddle on the street. I was sick. I didn't have a second to waste. Hiding between someone's garage and the car in their driveway, cooking it in a spoon not even a block from where I bought it, rationalizing that it was safe because the cook would kill any bacteria. Addict mentality. Filthy puddle water directly into my vein.

I went to rehab because there was no heroin in Toledo and I was in pain. I was getting clean whether I wanted to or not. I figured I might as well go to rehab.

***

I entered and bailed on rehab so many times, it was another part of the routine. Betray someone's trust, usually my mom's,

---

[12] Bic is a lighter brand you can find in every carryout and gas station in America.

promise to go to rehab, go to rehab, bail on rehab, repeat. One of those times when I just got out of rehab, I was immediately ready to use again but I didn't have my gear. I needed a syringe. In Toledo, you have your mailmen, policemen, and firemen, like anywhere else. Us addicts also had a needleman.

I went to his place, a big 2-story house on the east side. No lights, power, or water. It's not there anymore. It was condemned and demolished. The guy who lived there was a diabetic. I don't know if it was even his house or if he was squatting, but he was always home and he always had clean needles. He was *the* guy for clean needles. He had boxes and boxes of them, more than he needed. His place was like a drug-addict Walmart, with people coming in and out all day, paying $5 for a clean syringe. This dude made good money doing this. The place was big enough that you could even rent out rooms for an hour, for the night, whatever you wanted.

My guy held court at a small table in his kitchen, where he sat with a pristine box of beautiful unblemished syringes. Those needles were the only clean thing in the house. I paid him the five bucks and asked, "Hey, man, is it cool if I do this here?"

"Sure. That's another five dollars."

I gave him another five and he added, "You can use one of my chairs for 5 minutes."

$60 dollars an hour. Must be one hell of a chair. I pulled out a chair at the table, sat down, and got busy with my Bic barbeque. The place had a very open floor plan, and from where I was sitting, I had a perfect view of every room on the main floor: the adjoining dining room, the bedroom on the other side, and the bathroom.

It was easy to spot the bathroom because it didn't have a door on it and a guy was taking a shit. This house did not have running water. The guy wasn't having an easy time of it, either. One more side effect of opiates is constipation. I wonder how much the Needle Man charged for the toilet?

In the living room, a couple people were sitting on the floor smoking crack. On the other side, I could see a hooker was using the bedroom as her business office and was in the middle of entertaining clients. She looked beat up. She looked like 80 years crammed into a 40-year-old body. I don't know why she left the door open. Unlike the bathroom, that room actually had a door.

I had a moment, a brief moment, where I noticed myself. Those moments happened all the time, but I could usually push them out of my mind quickly. This time… I don't know. This time I really noticed what I was doing. As the spoon started getting hot I see that I am about to re-enter this world by choice. I am electing to be at this house, around these people, to be just like these people. I already detoxed. The hard part was over, right? I could just walk out right now. It was like seeing my future by climbing inside the crystal ball.

I looked at that nightmare and then I shot up anyway.

Chapter 14: Faith

It's hard to be a person of faith when you're an addict. You can't pray that dope baggies will fall from the sky like manna from Heaven. You can't expect a preacher to lay hands on you and instantly cure you of dope sickness. You can ask God to open the jail cell and let you out, but it never worked for me. The apostles were lucky that they got to see the miracles. Faith isn't as easy for the rest of us who came after.

I don't know if I would call myself a traditionalist, but sometimes traditions are traditions for a reason. Sometimes the tradition is so old, we forget why we even started doing it.

Meetings have traditions. You have your support group, people who are there in case you start slipping who you can call, day or night, and get help like they're your own personal 911. Meetings have a prayer they say most of the time. It's so well known that people who have never been to a meeting will recognize it.

God, grant me the serenity, to accept the things I cannot change, the courage to change the things I can, and the wisdom to know the difference.

Many people don't even realize that The Serenity Prayer isn't in the bible. It's *that* well-known.

Meetings are confessions to peers, instead of priests. Peers are the few people who will really understand what it is you are going through, the people who have done things just as bad or worse, and who are in no place to judge you as less than they are.

You give yourself over to a higher power, whatever that means for you.

I'd gone to more meetings than I could count but I didn't get it. I didn't see what any of this was for. I didn't see how any of this was going to help me. I knew better. I wasn't going to commit to a program, even though it's helped millions of people. That stuff is for you, not me. I'm different. I'm special. I was going to do it Matt's way, a way that had always failed me every time I tried it, 100% of the time. But I had an ego. That's the curse of succeeding early and often. I already had it all figured out. I actually believed that crap, even as a cop was cinching handcuffs around my wrists. What do I need a higher power for? I have it all under control.

I'll say it again. Addicts lie… to themselves most of all.

I was raised to believe in God. I was raised Catholic. And while I was using, I guess you could call me agnostic, meaning I was on the fence. I wasn't willing to commit to faith, but I wasn't an atheist, either.

When things come easy as a kid, it can be a curse. I know that sounds strange. It sounds like a person who had everything is complaining about how good they had it. But hear me out for a second. When you come up and things come easy for you—school, sports, making friends, meeting girls—it can make you weak. Spiritually weak. I mean that in two senses of the word: spirit, meaning your ability to emotionally overcome and endure, and also spirit meaning the intangible part of us that connects us to the divine.

I was great at sports. My academics were impeccable. I was lucky with girls. Honestly, the only thing I've ever failed at is using drugs successfully. And I've failed at it 100% of the time. When it comes to intoxicants, I am the 2008 Detroit Lions. It is an 0-16 season, every season. A lot of other failures and pain came from that one.

I've tried different substances. I've tried taking them in different ways. It doesn't matter. I can't do it. Some people can. But I can't. It's because of how I push things, because of my extreme personality, and because of my competitiveness. You chug a beer? Cool. I'll chug two beers.

When everything goes your way for a long time, it's easy to think everything is just *supposed* to go your way. It's easy to think that this is the ordinary state of things. Just like gravity pulls things down, and the sun always rises in the morning, you accept that this is just the way it is and always will be.

It's not.

Everything we have, every gift and blessing and bit of luck we have, it's all on loan. It's ours until it's taken back or we take it for granted and let it get away from us. When you remember that your time with it was a gift that you were borrowing, then giving it back doesn't hurt. You enjoyed it while you had it, and you feel gratitude towards Whoever loaned it to you. But sometimes people borrow something for long enough that they forget it's not theirs. They feel entitled to it. They forget it's only in their possession because of the kindness of someone (or Someone) else. And when that kind person takes it away, you don't thank them for the time they gave you. You resent them.

That was me. I was jaded. How could God do this to me? Imagine that. The unmitigated hubris of a man blaming God for putting a needle in his arm. I believed that God abandoned me when anyone half as smart as me could see that it was the other way around. I started this chapter by saying it's hard to be a person of faith when you're an addict. Maybe I have that backward. Maybe it's hard to be an addict when you're a person of faith.

This is a really common attitude. There is a chapter in The Big Book of Alcoholics Anonymous called *We Agnostics*. There's a line that asks, "Who are you to say there is no God?" Something makes the sun come up and go down every day, and it wasn't Matt Bell. But I didn't get that. Not yet. It took 10 or 11 more times in rehab before I actually understood that chapter.

Earlier, I said I worshiped the needle, and I meant it. People lose faith when their faith lets them down. When the faithful are abandoned. When the congregation and leaders weren't there when you needed them most. When you trusted the wrong priest, or donated to a charlatan. Heroin was a faith that did nothing *but* let me down.

After years of this, I started losing faith in it.

Chapter 15: I Met A Girl, Then My Son

On my tenth or eleventh rehab, I finally decided I'd give meetings a try. I wasn't fully signed on, but I told myself I would go to meetings, at least.

My life was a failure. I was letting down myself and everyone who cared about me. But remember what I said before about meetings. Meetings are full of other people who understand you, have been through the same shit as you or worse, and who aren't going to judge you. At the meetings, I met someone who understood. Someone who accepted me. We'd already spilled some of our darkest moments in a room full of other people. There weren't any secrets between us. I mean, imagine if your first couple dates with someone were just telling your date every bad thought and deed you ever did, and they were okay with all of that. That's a pretty intense context to meet someone. That was the environment where I met her. And she was cute, too.

We started talking. We started dating. A few months into dating, we decided to get pregnant. That's not usually how the story goes. Usually, it's an accident, or people get married first.

My friends weren't talking to me anymore. My mom didn't trust me. I had nobody except her. I wanted normalcy. When every day is a struggle, even just an hour of boredom sounds like a gift. I didn't even need to be a ball player anymore. Man, I'd be happy just stirring some Kraft macaroni & cheese powder into noodles while listening to my kids argue about whose turn it is to play Nintendo, while my wife told me about her day at work. Just one hour of that would be Heaven.

I wanted a real life back. Many failing marriages believe that adding a child will save them. I think I had a similar attitude. I wanted a wife. I wanted a kid. I wanted to make a normal, happy life that would keep me normal and happy. I wanted what I had when I was a kid, back when I was happy, back before my dad died. I wanted love. Real love.

It doesn't work that way, though. Having a son and wife wasn't going to save me. That was backward thinking. It was my duty as a father and husband to protect them. I wanted to be that man, but I wasn't ready to be that man. I wasn't taking the process at its own pace. I wanted to skip steps and go straight to normal. I ruined a lot of things, but the most important thing I destroyed was my relationship with my mom. Maybe I could start a new family and get it right this time. I wanted to get back what I'd lost, like a gambler going double-or-nothing at the blackjack table.

Jan 17th, 2011—13 months after meeting—our son Jackson was born. We got married a few months later.

I wasn't ready. I thought I was. I wanted to be. I was so excited to be this beautiful kid's dad. But I wasn't good yet.

I got sober and stayed "sober." I use quotation marks because I was taking suboxone, which is sort of like methadone, but I didn't have to go to a clinic every day. I was working out. I was healthy. I had a good job landscaping for Black Diamond. I was doing well. I made enough money that I could even step out and start my own business. I offered a good deal through Groupon that blew up. I got a lot of customers up front and made good money, and I was able to make new customers and develop business relationships with them by showing them that I was worth sticking with. It was looking like the old Matt magic was back.

Remove heroin and things just seemed to work out. Funny how that works.

I had jobs coming in that took me all over town. Sometimes it took me to the East Side. It took me near some of my old haunts, the places I used to buy from. Places I used to hang out. It had me feeling nostalgic. It was like the smell of McDonald's French fries. That company must have some amazing chemists because that smell does not exist anywhere else. Sure, you can smell fries at any diner or burger place. But McDonald's fries smell different. When you smell McDonald's fries, you don't want to get fries from Burger King or Wendy's. You want *those* fries. Just being back in that neighborhood, I could smell it every day.

***

It's hard to understand addiction if you aren't from that world. Here's the best way I can describe it that almost everyone understands.

An addiction is like a shitty ex. I bet everyone reading this book has a crazy ex that they couldn't quit, or had a friend who had a crazy ex.

The shitty ex. She's crazy. She's hot. She's manipulative. She is amazing at sex. And she will fuck up your life. She will accuse you of cheating for no reason, only for you to find out actually she's the one who's been cheating. She'll trash your Xbox when she gets mad at you. She'll call the cops on you and make up reasons when the police come. Then she'll attack the police while they arrest you for the crime she accused you of.

Even when you've had enough of her, and you finally pack up your stuff and leave, she's still around. She's in your head. She texts you sometimes. You want to answer, but you don't. You keep hearing about her from your mutual friends and acquaintances. She's out of sight, but she's not out of mind. She haunts you. And after a while, after the stress of her insane nonsense has died down, you start to remember the good times. Remember the good times? Remember the reasons you were with her? After a while, you mostly remember the good times. And one day, like a clairvoyant, she texts you like she knows you just forgot the bad times. This time, you text back. Just that one mistake brings you 80% of the way back to her. She gets to talking. She's a liar. You know she's a liar. You know that. But she tells you it'll be different this time. Somehow, you believe her. Somehow, you imagine this time it'll work.

It won't work.

That's what addiction is: a shitty ex-girlfriend you can't seem to quit. One drink, one puff, one snort, that's all it takes and she's on the phone talking to you, telling you in a sultry voice how much she misses you, how badly she wants to fuck you, how badly she needs you back. And you believe her. She talks like she's DTF because she's always down to *fuck you up*.

***

I was "clean" for two years. Two good years. Then I relapsed.

There was no instigating event. There was no emotionally complex moment. I just missed it. I just wanted to get high again. Most importantly, I thought that this time I could control it. I thought I could use and keep everything I had built: my marriage, my beautiful son, and my business. That's the problem with the Matt magic. It came with hubris. Every time.

The lies started again, the lies I told myself… *It was different back then. I can make it work this time. I know what went wrong last time. I won't repeat those mistakes. I got this. I can handle it.*

***

There's this old poem, Casey at the Bat.[13] It's a poem about baseball that's almost as old as baseball itself. If you haven't heard it, I'll give you the short version: a legendary baseball player steps up to bat. He's so cocky, he lets the first two pitches

---

[13] https://www.youtube.com/watch?v=erfSed2MUsA&t=3s

soar past him, so he starts with two strikes. Then he swings and misses.

Failing is never fun, but you can fail with dignity. But failing after you've been bragging, after you've been styling on someone, peacocking, and clowning... that's just embarrassing. You see it in the UFC all the time. As someone once told me, cockiness is a red light indicator. Get humble, or get humiliated.

This time wasn't different from any other time I used drugs. I wasn't spiritually fit to be back in the old neighborhood full of old temptations and opportunities. I wasn't working the steps. I wasn't going to meetings. In addition to taking suboxone, I was still drinking and smoking from time to time. Jackson's mom told me I shouldn't be doing that, but of course, Matt is fine. On the outside it might have looked like I was doing better, but on the inside I was a ticking time bomb. All I really had was money and bullshit I could tell myself.

Have you ever noticed how in those old Merry Melody cartoons, the tiny devil and angel on the shoulders look exactly like the character they're trying to influence? Those aren't actually devils and angels sent by Heaven and Hell. The devils and the angels fighting for Daffy Duck's soul are both Daffy Duck. It feels weird to type this right now, but that is very insightful by the animator.

I wasn't fully intending to get high. I was still just flirting with the idea. Maybe I'd already made up my mind, but I wasn't ready to admit it to myself just yet. I remember I was driving past East Broadway and saw a guy waiting at the bus stop. He was half conscious, hunched over, nodding because he could barely hold himself up. There was a cigarette limply hanging out of his mouth, the ash half as long as the cigarette itself.

Most people see that and they think something like, "That's sad," or, "This city is going to shit," or, "That guy better stay the hell away from me." Addicts are different. I didn't think any of that stuff. I saw that guy and thought, "Damn. That guy's got a good high going on." It's like when you are seated at a restaurant you've never been to. You pick up the menu, but then you see a waiter serve another table with something that looks amazing. You put down the menu because that's what you want.

I saw him and I pulled into a parking lot right away, got out, and approached him.

"Hey, man. You're high," I said.

He barely registered I was there. He looked in my direction, but he was somewhere else. Somewhere that I wanted to be.

"I'm not a cop," I assured him.

He still barely noticed me.

"I've got money. I'll buy you more if you get some for me, too."

He started paying attention.

It felt spontaneous, but thinking back on it, it really wasn't. I'd spent weeks talking myself into it. The angel on your shoulder is always right, but the devil on your shoulder is oftentimes the better salesman.

My instinct was right when I saw him. I could see that the guy on the bus bench was next-level high. I didn't know why. Not yet. He didn't take me to get heroin. There wasn't any heroin. Remember that cartel plug with a ton of guns and money? After he was busted, all the heroin dried up and it never came back.

The guy on the bench introduced me to fentanyl.

That's how I ruined my life the second time. Only this time, I had a wife and a son.

Just like that, I was back. Like that song by Mobb Deep goes, *"Ain't no such things as halfway crooks."*

Chapter 16: Everything I Wanted

The addict who's been sober for a while is at serious risk of overdosing. I said earlier that drugs literally damage your brain. Those injuries can and do heal, but only if you don't pick at the scab. The healing process is your body returning to its ordinary tolerance. When someone in recovery has stayed sober for a while picks up a needle and fills it with the same amount of dope they used to use, back when they used daily, they're going to give themself a lethal injection. Their body is not calibrated to handle what they used to be able to handle.

When addicts first come out of rehab—after they've detoxed, after they've started healing—they are in danger; if they relapse and try to go back at full speed, it can kill them. The complete stranger at the bus stop who was having a good high didn't take me to get heroin. He took me to get fentanyl, which you probably know is a whole other level of strength. If I had been completely clean, healed, and recalibrated, it probably would've killed me. I was still on suboxone. My brain had not fully healed yet because I was technically still taking an opioid every day. The massive dose wasn't a complete shock to my system. Earlier in this book I mentioned some of the cons of methadone and suboxone. In this case, suboxone probably saved my life.

Fentanyl was everywhere. When I got back to the game, you couldn't find heroin. It had become a rare boutique product. The War on Drugs started in 1971 and couldn't stop heroin. Fentanyl did.

***

My Groupon money evaporated. My business went away. I needed money fast, so I sold off my equipment, piece by piece, cannibalizing my business. I destroyed my ability to make good, regular money. Everything I'd worked for vanished into my arm.

My wife was in recovery. She knew the symptoms. Maybe she didn't want to see what was happening. Not at first. She was never a full-blown addict like I was. She had a pill problem for a few months, told her parents, and they sent her to rehab. But she'd been to the meetings. She knew the signs and knew something was up. And she knew me.

One night when she came home from work, she said to me, "Log into your bank account." We had a joint account and I had my own personal account. She meant my personal account.

"I don't remember the password." Addicts always lie.

"Reset the password, then. I know something's going on."

I did. I signed in. Her face dropped when she saw the screen. My account should have had about $80,000 we'd earned and saved. It had $6 left in it.

"Fuck you, you piece of shit! Fuck you for ruining this family!" She was right about that.

She took Jackson and left. She filed for divorce the next day and pulled up with her dad and uncle in two U-Hauls. I sat in my car and watched from across the street as she moved everything out of our home. Our whole life was placed into trucks, and a few hours later, it was gone. Just like that. At the time, I was mad at her. It felt like she was taking everything from me. Of course, that's the *exact opposite* of how it really was. Addicts always lie. They lie to themselves most of all.

I had no right to be mad at her. She did the best thing she could. She was protecting her baby. She wouldn't let me talk to our son or see him. She did the right thing. I was so mad, but when you're living wrong, the right thing feels like persecution.

I thought I had it. This is exactly what I told myself wasn't going to happen. After they were gone, I sat alone in that condo. I looked at the empty space that used to have the couch where we sat together and watched TV. I looked at the empty kitchen where we used to cook dinner. I listened to the quiet where I used to hear my son laughing, saying his first words. I lived in an empty condo filled with memories for two more months until they evicted me.

After Jackson's mom left, I lost our home, I cannibalized my business. I did it again. I had everything I wanted, *twice*, and I destroyed it, *twice*.

I went to the one place that would always take me back no matter what. I went back to Mom. My wife had to protect her baby. My Mom had to protect hers. She was always there for me, no matter how much I lied and disappointed her. I always had a place to land.

Chapter 17: I Go White-Collar

Addicts have a powerful entrepreneurial spirit. Imagine being homeless and waking up in the morning, with $2 in your pocket. A silent clock is ticking. You have to generate revenue within the next few hours before you start getting sick. This might mean hustling a ride from a stranger, who looks naive to get across town to Dick's Sporting Goods to steal something. Then you have to find somebody to sell it to, which might mean a 3-hour walk. Then you need to get that cash to a dealer. If your dealer isn't at home or isn't answering their phone, you will track that person down like a bloodhound, desperate to give them your money. All the while, you're dodging all the cops and enemies you earned in this town.

A few hours later, you will have to do this again. Tomorrow you'll do the same thing. Being an addict is a lot of work. Most people aren't up to it.

As the saying goes, work smarter, not harder. While I was at my mom's, I figured out how to use my entrepreneurial energy to make money on the internet. It wasn't a tech startup, exactly. I created a website and sold fake IDs. I even had a YouTube channel for marketing it. The internet really was the Wild West back in those days.

The thing is, I never actually sold anyone a fake ID. They paid me, but I never sent them the ID. The thing about crime is that there is no legal recourse when someone fucks you over. If someone steals a brick of heroin, you can't go down to the police station, file a report, give a statement, and hope your heroin is returned safely. Disagreements are resolved with violence or they are not solved at all. But by using the internet, I put a digital barrier between me and the people I ripped off. Even if they wanted to kick my ass or kill me, they wouldn't even know who

I really was, or where to find me. I could take the money, they couldn't do anything to me, and they couldn't tell the cops. It was a pretty great scam.

I'm not a tech expert or anything. I just went to GoDaddy, paid my nine bucks for the domain, and put together a very simple one-page website. I already had some experience with website building because I built one for my former landscaping company. On my YouTube channel, I showed my gear, trying to make it look as legit as possible. *Here are my high-end printers in my state-of-the-art ID-producing laboratory.* I showed pictures of IDs that I didn't make, photos I just grabbed off the internet as proof that I could create an ID for any US state. I blurred out the name and address as though I were protecting the identities of my clients.

I had a virtual phone number with a bogus Google voicemail. I had people from all over the world calling me. One of my biggest payoffs was a sex trafficker from Vegas who needed 30 IDs for women. He didn't tell me what he did for a living. He didn't need to. He sounded like a pimp, and when you need 30 IDs for women in Vegas, all between the ages of 19 and 21, it's easy to figure out what they're up to. I even gave him a bulk discount. Of course, he never received any of the IDs.

"Customers" paid through MoneyGram or Western Union, with half the deposit upfront. I took the deposit and told them I would send them a receipt of the tracking confirmation, and then they would send me the rest. They always sent the full deposit. Then I blocked them. I never sent them anything. There was a part of me that even felt good about it. I knew that whoever was taking these IDs was up to no good. This wasn't just 17-year-old kids trying to get IDs to buy beer. A sick addicted mind always latches on to any justification they can, any moral loophole to help them live with their behavior. I actually imagined it as though I were teaching these ne'er-do-wells a lesson. That's what you get. I'm like a Heroin Robin Hood, stealing from the criminals and giving to my drug dealer.

There are a lot of skills a person can learn that can be used for good or evil. A marine sniper can use the same skill set for bagging Nazis in France, or to assassinate JFK. In my case, maybe it was a little bit of both.

That was the same rationalization I used when I was stealing metal. If I saw a cast aluminum grill left out, I'd think, "They should know better. They should know what cast aluminum is worth." You could think of me as a security consultant who you didn't hire, and I chose my own price.

That was my life for a while. Wake up at Mom's house, walk down to the carryout around the corner and pick up my easy MoneyGram cash. It sure beat hustling metal and dodging cops. I was a white-collar, work-from-home tech entrepreneur.

***

Business slowed down. When your business is conning people, there isn't a lot of repeat business. When things were tight, I sold my phone. Just like I sold my lawn equipment. No consideration for the long term. I was always living to get through today. Every time I was in a pinch and I could sell my money-making tools, I always did. Every time. I kept sacrificing things that were really valuable in life to get me what I wanted right now. My business. My college education. My sports career. My nest egg. My family. My wife. My son. If you were starving to death, you'd sacrifice your house for just a can of soup. That's how it felt. Always starving.

Once again, with no way to make money and no way to buy drugs, I went back to rehab. When I was back out, I returned to what I knew: boosting stuff.

***

My other scam was gift cards.

Everyone knows what the black market is, but there's this other place in between legitimate businesses and the black market; a gray market. That's where this kind of thing happens. Gift cards are essentially a money laundering system for the poor and working class. It's a blurry place where legal and illegal overlap.

As long as I had my phone, I had my gift card business. First, I'd rip off department stores. Higher-end stuff was the best. Places like Dillard's and Dick's Sporting Goods were some of my favorite spots. I would boost something and then come back later to return it as though I was a legitimate customer who made a legitimate purchase. "I'm sorry, I don't know what happened to the receipt." They couldn't give me straight cash without a receipt, but they would give me store credit in the form of a gift card. What the hell am I going to do with a Dick's gift card? Same thing as scrap metal. I would sell that gift card to someone else. Cards are almost as good as cash.

I would sell them to semi-legitimate businesses, the same kinds of places where you can buy phone cards from a man behind bulletproof glass. The kinds of places that do a lot of money orders. Places that look like brick cubes, located on corners where the pavement is chipped and peeling back and little sprouts of grass are poking through, and there's always at least one guy just hanging around outside… you don't know why he's there, but you know his reasons aren't good.

These places knew exactly how I was getting gift cards. They bought them for 50 cents on the dollar. $100 of Home Depot gift cards was worth $50 cash. Sometimes they'd take advantage. They knew I was an addict. They knew everyone selling these things was a thief. Sometimes they just offered 30 cents on the dollar. What are you going to do about it? Are you going to go somewhere else? You need the dope money more than I need a gift card to Cirilla's.[14]

The same places would take EBT charges for items you're not allowed to spend EBT on.[15] Just like with the gift cards, they double the price in cash for the card's value. For example, a guy takes his girlfriend's EBT to one of these skeezy carryouts. The guy behind the counter knows the deal and rings it up as $40 of groceries, and hands his customer a $20 half gallon of Mohawk vodka. I did that too. Not for vodka, but I could sell my food stamps for cash. I could take a dealer to the grocery store and hook them up with $300 worth of groceries and they'd pay me with $50 of heroin.

In '97, the government pulled disability benefits for addicts and alcoholics. The cards are supposed to be for groceries only. They wanted a better system where they could give the benefits to people more trustworthy than an addict, someone like my mom. But of course, people found a way to abuse that system too, and worked around it. How do you help people who won't help themselves? How do you help people who will take advantage *every single time?*

***

Over at this carryout near where I was using (and sometimes sleeping) they were throwing out a bunch of phones that were too old to sell. Old Blackberries and shit. Junk. The guy was taking them all out to the dumpster, so I offered to take them off his hands. He shrugged and let me have the box. I figure I could sell them for maybe $5 a pop.

I walked around looking for customers. I saw some young guys riding around on bikes. They might have been in high school.

---

[14] Cirilla's is a chain of stores that sells "adult novelties."
[15] Electronic Benefits Transfer, or what they used to call "food stamps." These are debit cards that can only be used to purchase food.

Hard to tell. Some kids who come up rough try to look older than they are. But some older guys are so damaged, they are adults who are still 14 mentally. Kids don't know shit, right? Maybe I can talk them into buying one of these phones.

"Hey, you wanna buy a phone?"

The kids came up and browsed through my box. When each kid had a phone they liked in each hand, they all split in different directions. They didn't even signal each other to go. I guess they'd done this sort of thing before. In my head, they weren't stealing garbage phones. In my addict brain, they were taking off with my next high. Six phones at $5 is enough dope to keep me from getting sick, and these punks just took that from me.

I couldn't go in three directions, so I picked one and chased after him. I wasn't in shape like I used to be, but I was quick enough. I caught him in an alley. I pinned him against a wall, one hand on his neck, and I stopped myself. *What the fuck was I doing? Am I about to choke this kid for fucking garbage that was about to go into a dumpster less than half an hour before?* I let go of him. He picked himself back up and started running again, calling back at me, "My brother's gonna fuck you up!" or some dumb shit like that. Maybe it sounded intimidating in his head, but to me, it came off like, "My dad can beat up your dad."

That was a moment to reflect on myself. I almost seriously fucked someone up for a pound of cheap Korean plastic and circuitry that was obsolete 10 years ago. It's hard to think straight when you're on the clock. The sickness is always on its way. The sickness never takes a break. It never takes days off. It is always coming for you. I didn't have time to reevaluate my life. I only had time to hustle the rest of those phones.

Chapter 18: Jail

I don't remember exactly how many times I've been to jail, but as best as I can remember it was 13 times. I was in and out all the time. After a while, it all just starts to blend.

Every time I went to jail, I had to detox. My entire life was organized around never, ever going through withdrawal, always being one step ahead of the sickness. In jail, there's nowhere to run.

Detoxing in jail is the worst. The lights are bright as fuck. The food is disgusting. The bed is an inch of mattress—compressed down by thousands of guys who laid on it before you—on a wire rack. It's loud. It's echoey. And no one—I mean, no one—gives a shit about your pain. Dopesick fuckups like you are in and out every day. You're as eventful as seeing a Toyota Prius in a Starbucks drive-thru.

Jail is scary. In jail, there are rules. They aren't written down anywhere. No one tells you what they are. But believe me, they are *strictly* enforced, and not by the corrections officers. And every jail has different rules and different enforcers. You will learn the rules—usually the hard way—and you will obey them.

Sick as I was, I went to chow to eat, just to try to distract my mind from obsessing about heroin. I got in line, got my tray, got my food that met the legal minimum standards for inmate nutrition, and I found a seat. Most guys had their own hot sauce that they put on everything. With enough hot sauce or vinegar, you can fix almost anything. Hot sauce couldn't fix what ailed me, though. When you are dope sick, you aren't hungry. You can't even look at food, it makes you sick. Jail food makes you feel even more sick. I knew I had a few days more of this at least.

People setting down trays sounded intensely loud. The fluorescent tube lights were blinding. Every sense was dialed up to superhuman levels of sensitivity. So there I am, sick as fuck, with a tray of perfectly good food in front of me that I can't eat. I offered my tray up to someone. No good reason to waste it.

A kind soul saw me, came up to me, and gave me some much-needed advice.

"You can't give shit to people in here."

"Why not?"

"If you give something to someone, they'll think you want to fuck them."

"What?" It sounded insane.

"Or they're gonna think that you think they owe you something."

"Oh. Well shit."

"Someone in here hands you a candy bar, and you take it, they'll be back looking for you to give them something. And if you don't give it to them, they'll just take it."

He didn't need to explain what "it" meant. "Oh *shit*."

No normal person on the outside would ever think like that. No right-thinking person would turn down a candy bar because it would mean giving up your ass to a 300 pound dude with a terrifying nickname like Glove. Or maybe you offer your tray to Glove, and he ain't into all that, but everyone else saw you offer it to him like he's a punk, so now Glove has to fuck you up in front of everyone just so everyone knows he doesn't turn tricks for trays.

That's how it is. There are rules. The rules are violently enforced. Consider yourself lucky if someone tells you what the rules are before you break them.

That was in Lucas County, one of the first times I was arrested. I was still a kid. In my mugshot, I was even wearing my University of Toledo shirt. I didn't know the rules yet.

Even after a dozen more arrests, I was still pretty new to it. I'd still spent less time there than most of the other inmates.

***

I cried one time. Not for nothing. I was on the phone in one of the common areas, talking with my mom, asking her to come bail me out, and she said, "No." One of the first no's she should've given me, but if I wasn't out, I would be stuck there until I could see a judge. And it was a Friday.

Some guys playing cards saw me and started yelling at me, "Look at that little bitch!" And everyone nearby who hadn't noticed looked my way and started laughing at me. There are rules, and they are enforced by inmates, not guards. That's how I learned that crying is not allowed.

AA would come in once a week for people like me. I would go to meetings. I wasn't even trying to clean up. Maybe I thought it would look good for a judge. Maybe I was just bored. But after the meeting, an older dude approached me and asked if I was okay. Not in front of others, obviously. That's another rule: compassion is weakness. Weakness is against the rules.

"I know why you're in here. I've been through it, too. But you can't do that here. You can't cry in here. Understand, there are straight-up *killers* in here. They are *never* getting out of here, they are mad at the world, and they don't give a single *fuck*. One day if they are pissed about something, and they just want to take it out any way they can, and they see you looking weak and crying—with no colors and no friends—they might decide it's gonna be you that they take their frustrations out on. You wanna cry, go do it into your pillow, do it quietly, and make sure you are dry as a bone and your eyes ain't red before you get off your bunk."

He was right about the killers.

Here's the thing about prison. Most of them are tiered. The top tier is for the worst, scariest psychos. Your hard-as-fuck killers, serial rapists, and ride-or-die skinheads. Then there is the next tier for guys like me: addicts, petty thieves, and even white-collar criminals. This tier is for people who might run away if you give them a chance, but they aren't the type to murder their celly if guards don't keep them away from pencils. But jail is different. Jail is for *everybody*. There are guys like me, just waiting to get bailed out, and people there for misdemeanors. There are also some seriously scary dudes who are there waiting to get in front of a judge for a triple homicide. They are all mixed together.

I once bunked with a dude of that scary variety. He was all over the news when he arrived, too. He robbed a gas station for some prepaid phone cards and a couple boxes of Newports. The gas station isn't there now, but it was on the corner of Dorr and Secor. He waved his gun, made his demands, and when he had everything he asked for, he told the teller to turn around and then shot the guy in the head. He murdered someone for nothing.

This murderer was my bunkie for two months. And what really fucks me up is that he was a nice guy. We talked to each other. We got along. To think that a guy who was so easy to hang with could murder a stranger for cigarettes… I still can't wrap my head around that.

***

The fourth floor at Lucas County jail is where they put all the young little hood rat gangbangers. The second floor is where they kept the addicts. So on this one occasion, I have no idea why they put me on the 4th floor. Those guys were loud as fuck *all the time*, even late into the night they were rapping, joking, carrying on like this was some kind of fucked-up summer camp for sociopaths. And they would fight over everything, just whoop each other for the dumbest reasons. They fought all the damn time, all day, every day. And they were dirty. The 4th floor was filthy. *Lord of the Flies* would be a tropical resort by comparison.

The jail was overcrowded, which made people act even crazier than usual. I didn't even have a cell. I was on a stack-a-bunk in the common area. It looked like a YMCA housing hurricane refugees. I'd come back from my court appearance and someone had stolen my pillow, sheets, and my blanket. And they knew I was detoxing. I was so sick, I couldn't do something about it. And even if I was healthy, what am I supposed to do about 25 hood rat gangbangers clowning me? Am I gonna fight all of them? I tried to just sleep while I heard them snickering at me.

***

"Hey, yo, Drake!" They called me Drake because I'm light-skinned. Not the worst nickname I heard there. One of these guys had his own cell, and they waved me in. There were two others there with him, and those rooms were cramped enough with just two guys in them, so when I went in, we were packed in close enough I could feel them breathing.

"Drake. I can see you ain't feelin' well. So lemme help you out. Gimme your trays for the next week, and we'll give you this." He flashed a bag real quick, cautiously, like he didn't want the COs[16] to see what we were up to.

"Lemme see it."

"What the fuck?" He asked, very defensively. Too defensive for a guy trying to sell dope in a county jail. "I ain't showing you anything!" The way he was behaving, you'd think I'd asked to see his dick. "I don't know if you snitch or not! I'm offering to

---

[16] Corrections officers aka guards.

make you feel better! Do you want this or not?" A true humanitarian, this guy.

"Nah," I walked away.

"Hey hey, come back. I'll show it to you."

I went back in. He showed it to me. I don't know what the hell it was, but it was *not* dope. It looked like rolled-up pieces of paper in a sandwich baggie. I don't know how he thought that would ever work on a pro-tier addict.

"Nah, man. I'm not fucking stupid." But this time I couldn't leave. One of his buddies was behind me, blocking the exit.

"The fuck did you just say?"

"I said I'm not stupid, I don't want that, and I'm not trading my food for it."

Then they kicked my ass. Not a damn thing I could do about it. I'll say, though, they didn't fuck me up nearly as bad as they could have. They could've crippled me, killed me, done literally anything they wanted. It was 30 seconds at most, mostly body shots because they didn't want to fuck up my face if I didn't make them. If my face was busted, the staff would see and review the tapes.

I went to the ground, and they stomped me out a bit. It sucked, don't get me wrong, but it could've been a lot worse. They wanted me hurt just bad enough that I'd know how bad they *could* hurt me if they wanted to. They wanted me to know that I don't get to say no to them and their stupid scam.

"You better not fucking tell anyone about this."

I'm glad they told me that. That was another rule that no one tells you. He didn't just mean not to tell the guards. They meant to not tell *anyone*. That's how it was.

***

The boredom is overwhelming. Any job that distracts you is a blessing. You will read any book they give you, it doesn't matter. Working a kitchen or folding laundry isn't a chore, it's a gift, especially for someone like me who can't sit still. So I did some thinking, whether I wanted to or not.

I know a lot of people who have been locked up for possession or dealing or doing something else they shouldn't have been doing. People who had to experience withdrawals inside the concrete walls of the jail cell. Honestly, I've probably met at least a thousand people like this. They live their lives in fear of detox and then are forced to do it in the worst possible place. And then when they get out, they go right back to the needle. Out of literally thousands of people I've met, both when I was using and while I've been working in recovery, I've known two who actually took the opportunity to straighten themselves out while they were locked up. Incarceration in my experience has a 0.2% success rate with cleaning people up, even with all of the classes and resources that jails will offer inmates.[17] 0.2% of people got clean and *stayed* clean *because* of jail.

So what's jail for? What is even the point of locking up addicts?

They're three ways of looking at it.

1. Incarceration is a deterrent. You punish some people to warn other people not to repeat those mistakes.
2. Incarceration is for reform. You send people to jail or prison to give them time to reflect on their behavior, essentially giving them a "time out." It's called a penitentiary because you were supposed to use the time to be penitent.

---

[17] This is not a verified statistic. It's just my best guess from personal experience. Just take it to mean "barely anyone."

3. Incarceration is to remove criminals from society so that they can't abuse society with their crimes.

Based on my experiences in what I've seen, jail time isn't a deterrent for addicts.

Jail is definitely not for reform, given those numbers I just shared, and the recidivism rates that you can find for yourself on government websites. Incarceration is definitely not a therapeutic treatment for antisocial behavior. If anything, it's the opposite. You are locked in a small space with other thieves, addicts, and a lot worse. Jails and prisons are more like finishing schools for criminals where they can network, make friends, and learn more—and learn it faster—than they ever would on the streets.

There is not much to do while incarcerated besides talk. I could walk into that place with a GED in oxycontin and 3 months later I'd leave with a master's degree in heroin. I learned so much just by being around other people who were much more experienced than I was.

I'm not exaggerating when I say networking. I met a lot of guys inside. We talked about scams and stuff, only to meet up back outside and work that angle we came up with in jail. It's like Ocean's 11 during the planning session at the beginning of the movie. It's LinkedIn for people who want to do bad things.

It's not a deterrent. It's not reforming people. That leaves the last option, which simply removes people from society.

But it's not even good at that. For the smaller crimes like possession, criminals are removed for maybe 4-12 weeks, just to return back and do exactly what they were doing before.

So what is the point of this? What is this even for? If you lock up a murderer for life, at least that third point makes sense; they're removed from society so they can't hurt anyone. Most people probably don't care if a murderer feels penitent. Most people who commit murder are well aware of the risk and either commit the murder in the heat of passion, or they think they are smart enough to get away with it.

But for addicts, what is even the point of this?

The ugly, and sometimes unpopular answer is very simple. Money. It's just business. A huge business. Prisons, jails, and the whole judicial system are all broken. They call it corrections, but what the fuck are they correcting? Who is getting corrected by sitting in a cage for a month? Are any of those guys on the 4th floor acting correctly?

There is plenty of research on the basic psychology of positive reinforcement, negative reinforcement, modeling, and actually teaching someone something. Nothing that the psychological discipline has learned about the human mind is being put to work in these places.

***

I got divorced while I was in jail. I couldn't even go to the court date. The whole thing was finalized and I couldn't do anything. I couldn't fight it if I wanted to. And even while I was locked up, I had to pay child support. Those payments started adding up, and I was already in arrears. The minute I got out of jail, I was already behind. A cop could have picked me up at any time. As soon as I was free, I already had a warrant for non-payment of child support.

This is another thing that can get people really stuck inside the system.

My ex and our child need money. That's a given. It's my responsibility to provide that money. That's also a given. I wasn't being a good father or husband. Even if I wanted to be, I was in jail, and there's nothing I could do about it.

From the state's perspective, *someone* has to pay for this kid. It *should* be the father, but if dad doesn't pay, the state is going to have to step in and pay. What happens if dad doesn't pay, or can't pay? Are they going to make dad pay? How? The way they always make people do things: they throw him in jail as a punishment. They go to corrections to be corrected. So now, not only is no money going towards the child, and the state has to pay for the kid as a surrogate father, but the state's also paying for the dad to be in jail. In the end it costs *more* money.

Go to any jail cell in America, and you will meet a lot of guys who are there for not paying child support. Every single time. Because they know this is just going to cost them more money, it's almost always a book and release. They waste the cops' time to jail him, a judge waves their finger at the deadbeat dad, and then go back to things as usual. What does that do? What is the point of this? It would be cheaper just to pay the guy to not have more kids.

It's probably no coincidence that you'll hardly meet any men in jail who knew their father. I was the rare exception. I promise you that most of those knuckleheads on the 4th floor wouldn't be in there if they'd had a dad like Roy.

***

I had a conversation with a jail case manager not too long ago and I asked her, "What percentage of people are directly or indirectly in jail for something to do with drugs or alcohol? Whether they were selling it, fighting someone for it, robbing someone for it, got a DUI, got in a drunk driving accident, sex crime…"

She estimated about 95-98%.

There are some total sickos in the world, and if drugs never existed, they'd still be serial killers and rapists. Jeffrey Dahmer is probably one of those people, but even he had a serious alcohol problem and was drunk as shit when he was murdering those men.

With all this shit, there are always drugs and alcohol involved.

I never got better in jail. I never even had a conversation with a social worker, judge, lawyer, administrator, guard, or advocate about what I was going to do when I got out. I never discussed going straight or strategizing about the better life that we were going to live. Not *once*. It was the opposite. Instead of saying goodbye, the corrections staff would always say, "See you back here soon."

I barely remember the staff. They all just… sucked. Frankly, they're assholes. They're not rooting for you. They're jaded. They just don't care. I was arrested 13 times in four states and I never saw anything that looked like penitence, correction, or rehabilitation. The truth is, they can't do those things—not because they don't want to—but because they don't know how.

Take a dog, any breed you like, and imagine that the dog misbehaves. Let's say a golden retriever. Everyone loves golden retrievers. The dog pees on the carpet or growls at your elderly grandmother. Bad dog! Imagine taking that dog and putting it in a kennel as punishment. Inside, the dog is in close proximity to three rottweilers who were trained by their former owners to fight. Imagine that a golden retriever is released from the kennel 6 months later. Do you think you're getting the same dog back? Do you think that your golden retriever is coming back frisky and friendly and good with kids? That dog will come out pitiful and submissive, jumping at any sound, growling at anything it interprets as a threat. Or the dog comes out more violent and aggressive than it was before, just as mean as its rottweiler cellmates because it had to be that mean to survive. More than anything else, the golden retriever will still pee on the carpet or growl at grandma, because it hasn't been taught how to behave properly. Sometimes the dog doesn't come out at all, killed by those rottweilers in a scrap over some dry kibble.

It's easy to understand when we're talking about dogs. So why is it so difficult to understand when we're talking about humans?

Chapter 19: I'm Not An Alcoholic

There are brief moments of clarity that appear while you're high. That probably sounds strange, but when you are hurting and chasing $20 to get your next fix, the fix is all you think about. When you first pushed the plunger on the needle and sailed off, you had a brief moment's peace from that chase. Once the hurting was gone, my thoughts could return to some semblance of normalcy. Strange to say it, but numerous times I had deep revelations when I was high. Not because I was high, but because in those clear moments I could actually meditate and think about who I was and what I was doing. It's funny that the times I felt that I most sincerely wanted to get clean was while I was high.

When the high ends, and you feel the tug of your neurotransmitters begging you to get some more, that kind of reflection and clarity vanishes until you can push that plunger again.

In those moments I would think about Jackson.

You wouldn't know it by the way I was acting, but having a son changed things for me. It's one thing to destroy my own life, to break my mother's heart regularly, and ruin what could have been a real marriage. But now there was a person in the world who didn't have a father. I had the best father in the world, squandered the nest egg and wisdom he gave me, and he was taken from me too soon. I can't even imagine what it would be like if he was never in my life to begin with. That was the future I was creating for Jackson. A future just like all those guys I met in jail.

A brief high and calm, then the crushing guilt and remorse, followed by promises to myself that I would do the right thing. But then the high faded and I needed to go find $20 again.

***

After one of my jail detoxes, I was back living with Mom. I found myself a decent job, and even had a car. I was doing pretty well. I was back on the right track. I was using the money I made to chip away at all the fines and child support that I needed to catch up on. It earned me enough goodwill with my ex that she was finally willing to let me see Jackson again. That's why I did it. That's why I *could* do it. It was all to win back my son.

I didn't get a lot of time with Jackson at first, which was understandable. My ex knew what recovery was like. She knew how easy it was to slip back. She knew that addicts always lie. She was being smart. I saw Jackson just once a week to begin. I didn't even need a court-ordered chaperone. Thankfully, Jackson's mom never made me do anything like that. We eased into it when she saw that I was walking the walk, doing what I was supposed to be doing. Cautious, but optimistic.

That was in 2013. I started getting tattoos. My tattoo artist loved to drink, and addiction loves to proselytize. I started just having a few drinks with him. We developed a little bit of a tradition, going out and playing pool as soon as he finished up on one of my tattoos. It was a regular Friday thing. Get a tattoo, get drunk. I was having fun. I remember when I was a kid trying alcohol for the first time and thinking this is so much fun. It was like that again. Opiates were never fun, and the longer I was on them, the less fun they were. But beer? Beer was fun.

I wasn't on any medications anymore. I wasn't taking methadone or suboxone. In my mind, that meant I was 100% clean. But I started to drink. It started with just seeing friends at bars. I figured this was normal. I can drink and stay normal. People can drink and live normal lives. I did… for maybe 3 to 6 months.

You already know where this is going. You can probably see it happening in slow motion. I should have been able to see it. I didn't see it, or I didn't want to see it, but I think everyone reading this book already knows how this chapter ends. It's gotta be frustrating for you just to see it typed on a page. Imagine what it was like for everyone who loved me and gave me more chances than I deserved.

One of the things about alcohol is that it reduces your impulse control. It makes you easier to persuade, which is why people like to have business meetings over cocktails. With my guard down even more, I didn't turn down coke when it was offered. A little bit of coke perks you up, makes you focused, alert, and in the moment. If you do a lot of coke, it can make you feel tense and uptight. So you need to level off that anxiety with more beer. A lot of beer and you lose concentration, you start slowing down. So you need some coke to bring you back up. Coke gets you up, and beer brings you down. Gotta get up to get down.[18]

When I was a little kid, schools had us go to a drug education class to try and stop us from growing up to become exactly what I became. They talked about "gateway drugs." They reasoned that if someone smoked marijuana, they were more likely to try heroin than someone who never tried marijuana. Therefore, "Don't smoke marijuana, kids!" Funny. They didn't call alcohol a gateway drug, and I've never met a heroin-addict who didn't have a beer first.

You see, I didn't understand that I was an *addict*. I thought I was a *heroin* addict, not an alcoholic. Over the next nine months, I finally realized that I was addicted to *all* substances. It is not one thing for me. It is *any* mood or mind-altering substance.

I was still working. I was doing well enough that I could tell myself I was doing alright. Addicts always lie, especially to themselves. Like Rick James famously said on Chappelle's Show just six months before he died, "Cocaine is a hell of a drug."

---

[18] Coolio, "1, 2, 3, 4 (Sumpin' New)"

I was drinking so much it was disgusting. I was never a coke guy before. I liked downers. I liked alcohol. I liked weed. I liked opiates. Coke speeds you up. Coke was part of the new "sober" me. Coke is very expensive. Compared to cocaine, those other things are dirt cheap, practically free. I was doing lines as thick as my finger. I would snort a whole 8-ball in two lines. $150 up my nose, just like that. And I was doing stupid, stupid shit. My friends called me Hoover. They should've called me Kirby.

Alcohol and cocaine made me into the worst version of myself. I was a degenerate. Motorcycles. Tattoos. Punk rock. Booze and blow. Another phase. Another round of trying to invent myself, but thinking I was finding myself. I was like that my whole life. I would be a skater. Then I'd be into BMX. Then I was a jock. Then I was a prep. I was even emo for a week. It was like trying on other people's lives just to see how it feels. Most importantly, trying to be these people just to see how others responded to it. I always wanted approval, and I was always looking for new ways to be the cool guy. I wanted to fit in, but to also stand out. Maybe that's a contradiction.

***

One night I was on Facebook wasting time scrolling through the endless feed of bad memes and baby pictures from people I barely knew 10 years ago. I saw a picture and stopped. It was a photo of a girl I knew back in the day, from my sister school, St. Ursula. Monica. Damn. She wasn't a girl anymore, though. She posted some pictures of herself in Italy and she looked fucking amazing. I DM'd her and told her so. Believe it or not, that worked. I scored a date with Monica from St. Ursula. I cold-called her on Facebook after all those years and she took me up on my offer.

She had no idea what I'd been up to since high school. If she did, she probably would have blocked me.

She wasn't going to meet the Matt she thought she knew. She was about to meet rebel Matt, a carefree, don't-give-a-fuck hedonist with a dark past. I had turned into a player. I was that guy who was just out to hook up with someone else's girl. I wasn't there to find a single girl and make a connection. I was there to pick up a girl who was there with her man, while he watched powerless to do anything about it. If they tried to do anything about it, I would fight them. It didn't matter if I knew this guy, if I had a problem with him or not, or if I even liked his girl because I didn't care about her. I only wanted one thing. That "one thing" wasn't what you think, either. I wanted the challenge. I was a top competitor in a sex and violence biathlon. But most of all, I thought it was cool. Despite everything my father told me, I thought that the character I was playing, Mr. Steal-Yo-Girl, was what a real man was.

I was a piece of shit, and Monica had no idea who she was going on a date with.

I was angry. All the time. The thing about cocaine and alcohol: they don't always make people more angry, but they sure as hell never once made a person *less* angry. It's a near-perfect cocktail for violence. Cocaine makes you feel like Iron Man. Alcohol makes you too stupid to feel fear or pain. Anyone with some sublimated anger should never go near the stuff individually, let alone at the same time. I was miserable. If I could make others miserable, too? Good. They should feel miserable. That was my attitude.

I didn't used to be angry, and I didn't want other people to be unhappy. I *like* people. I was a likable guy, in no small part because it's easy to be likable when you like people.

The main place I went to was the Bier Stube. I went in there and—just like in the show—everybody knew my name.[19] I could walk in and there would always be friends to greet me. Everybody knew me. I fit in. But I also had to stand out. I had to be good at something. I needed to take someone's money and hustle them in a game of pool.. I needed to take someone else's girl. I needed to hook up with more than one girl on the same night, just to say I did. I would make her feel like I really was interested. I wasn't. I didn't even want her, so much as I wanted the conquest. I wanted to prove to myself that I *could* have her. It wasn't honest, even by hookup standards. I did it just for the challenge just so other people would know that I was the guy who could.

Pleasure-seeking and hedonism aren't wrong in and of themselves, but the way I was doing it always hurt other people. I went there to have a good time and it always meant making sure someone else *didn't* have a good time.

So that was the guy Monica was about to meet at Bier Stube on the Saturday night we scheduled our date.

It didn't go like that, though. The angry punk didn't show up for the date... Matt did. There was something about Monica. I didn't know what it was, exactly, but this girl was different. It's the kind of feeling you get from a woman where you need to see her again, just to figure out what that feeling is. I was myself with her. For the first time in a long time, I was myself. I missed that.

After our first date, I told my buddy the tattoo artist, "I'm gonna marry her, dude." I wanted to spend my life with her, learning about what the hell it was that made her special.

"She's just… right. She's good. She's a good woman. She's not like these other people." I didn't know it yet, but Monica was the kind of woman who made you want to be a better man. Not a

---

[19] Reference to the old sitcom Cheers, for any readers who are too young to know what I'm talking about.

cooler man. Not a man who fits. She made me want to be a *good* man. A man who was good enough to deserve her. There are a lot of things a father can teach their son about being a man. This is something only a very special woman can teach.

We really hit it off. She was college-educated. That doesn't always mean smart, but she was. She was *sharp*. She was put together. She had a good family. She was living life right. I was a bar-hopping man-whore making terrible money at a job I didn't care about, paying off child-support from my time in jail, and I had just saved enough money to move out of my mom's place and buy a tiny white Saturn I called The Q-Tip because it looked like the cotton end of a Q-Tip.

I got to be me with her. And she liked me.

***

I was dishonest with Monica from the start, because she was too good for me. I knew that. I didn't want *her* to know that. I was looking at an apartment on Douglas. I asked her to come along and check it out with me. I didn't show up in the Q-Tip. I showed up in my mom's Dodge Charger. I wanted to impress her. I felt ashamed of being who I was when I was with her. I wanted to be better. I wanted to be good enough for her. In the meantime, I faked it to make it.

You can't fake it forever.

We kept seeing each other. I still drank. I still partied. But I toned it down. Restraint wasn't my thing, but she inspired some in me. I wasn't the absolute barbarian I'd been just an hour before our first date. We'd go out and have some drinks, but we went home together. Just her and I, back to my place on Douglas. Rock-and-roll Matt didn't date, just hookups. He was about earning a high score. But that ended with Monica. After I met Monica, I was about Monica.

One night she got to see me drunker than she'd ever seen me before. I'd been out with the boys playing pool. Usually, I dialed it in when I was with her. Not that night. Monica was the brakes to my gas pedal. The brakes were a little soft that night.

I was hanging with friends and Monica back at my place. She excused herself to the bathroom. When she came out, the fellas had brought the cocaine out and laid out what we called "gaggers" on the table, which are stupidly large lines of blow. I figured it would be cool. It's just cocaine, right? It's not a *hard* hard drug, right? Monica will be cool with it, right?

Wrong.

She walked right up and swiped $100 of cocaine onto the floor.

"What the fuck is this?" she screamed. "This isn't you!"

Yes, it is.

"You're better than this!" she said.

No. I'm not.

When the girlfriend destroys your drugs and starts yelling, the party is over. My friends excused themselves fast.

That was a bad night.

***

As I write this book, I see a pattern. If I'm a good enough writer, maybe you've seen it, too. It's like the better things got for me, the more I wanted to go back to the needle. Something inside of me is always trying to get me to throw it all away again. And again. And again. I've already compared the habit to a crazy ex-girlfriend you can't forget. The habit is jealous. She doesn't want to see anything else make me happy. The habit thinks that only *she* can make me happy. The happier I got without drugs, the more love and success I found, the more the habit wanted me all for herself.

Things were going okay. I had it under control. *Matt is fine.* I got cocky again.

I knew some guys from Detroit a couple years back and gave them a call. The number still worked. I couldn't believe it. They set up a place to meet when I got off work. It was a social visit, but it was also a purchase. It was like the guy on that bus bench. The habit found me like we'd just accidentally bumped into each other at the grocery store. Out of nowhere. Just like that.

I couldn't tell you why I called. I guess the habit called me.

Memory is strange. I remember that night so vividly, even though I've forgotten details about things that should be more important. It was fall. Maybe November. Cold, dry air, already giving the tip of my nose pins and needles. I remember the time of night, my hands buried in my coat. I remember the street light perfectly. Every detail. The yellow glow and how it shined off the cars. I remember the quiet, with all the crickets and birds long gone. Just the occasional sound of a distant car, like an ocean wave. I remember being excited to see the guys from Detroit like these were old friends.

The guys pulled up in a car with windows tinted so dark they might as well have been painted black. I walked up. They cracked the window a couple inches.

"Money."

I slipped the cash in through the slit like it was a vending machine.

"Put your hand out."

I put my hand into the narrow gap in the window. I couldn't see what was on the other side. I felt someone put fentanyl chunks directly into my hand. Not a bag of drugs. Just straight drugs directly into my hand. It was so strange. Maybe they didn't have time to stop at the corner store for baggies.

Then my "friends" drove off. The way I remembered them, those guys were old friends. I guess I remembered it differently than how it really was. Like I said, memory is strange. Truth is, it was probably a new round of dope boys that were just manning the same phone.

I went back to my car with a palm full of opiates, got inside, and scrounged up something to place this stuff in. The best I had was a crumpled-up receipt from Kroger. Once my fentanyl was mostly secure, I drove to my next appointment.

I didn't want to get high. Not yet. I still had a dinner and movie date with Monica.

Chapter 20: The Worst Date Ever

Monica and I had a nice dinner at home. No, that's not true. It wasn't nice. Honestly, I was kind of an asshole. I wasn't interested in dinner. I just wanted to get high. I told her I wasn't feeling right, and suggested maybe she should leave. She wasn't happy about it, but she did. Date canceled.

As soon as she was gone, I headed for the bathroom to shoot up. I wasn't halfway there when I heard a knock on the door. I went back and opened it. It was Monica.

"No. You know what? This is bullshit. I'm eating dinner with you tonight. Deal with it." Date uncancelled. Like I said, Monica is special. Then we had dinner.

We picked out a movie. I don't remember what, but it didn't matter. You know how it is. We were on the couch, watching a movie, but you never expect to make it to the end of the movie. We started making out, getting intimate… but I couldn't. I was distracted. I couldn't think about Monica. All I could think about was another woman named fentanyl. She was right there in my pocket. I was fixated on it. All I wanted was to get it over with and get to the real date I had planned for tonight. I had this beautiful woman in front of me, but all I could think about was the next high.

Addiction is a controlling girlfriend. You have no say in anything. The relationship always gets sick. It gets abusive. It gets dangerous. The police get involved. Addiction really is that fucked up, psycho ex, and mine was in my pocket.

Monica could tell something was up. "What's wrong?"

"Nothing. I just gotta… I gotta use the restroom. I'm not feeling well." No woman ever takes that well, but it was the best line I had at the moment. "I think maybe it was something I ate."

When I was alone in the bathroom, I couldn't wait for her to leave. I had the whole kit there ready to go: needle, lighter, spoon, and a receipt wrapped around drugs. In a way, Monica gave me opium blue balls by not leaving the first time. I was ready to cook the second the door closed behind her, but I learned that Monica is not a woman you just cancel on. I figured I had to cook right there, get my high, and go back in and play it cool for the rest of the date. Maybe talk her into leaving. Maybe when I was high I'd look sick and my story would sell. I don't know. All I knew was I couldn't wait another second. The implements of the ritual got my blood pumping.

I cooked right there in the bathroom, Monica on the other side of the door, probably worried I had food poisoning, or worried that she did something to turn me off enough that I ran to the bathroom.

Do you remember a few chapters back, when I talked about the increased risk of overdose after getting clean and then relapsing? I switched from heroin to fentanyl, and the only reason I didn't OD that first time was because I was still taking suboxone and my body was still acclimated to opiates.

I was 100% clean from opiates. This time I wasn't on suboxone.

I OD'd on my date with Monica. It wasn't my first OD. But it was my worst.

***

My First OD

> My first OD was after rehab. I told my mom that rehab didn't pay for laundry and I needed her to bring me $10 in quarters every week. After 30 days, I was released from

rehab with $40 worth of quarters in my pocket. Addicts always lie.

I went back to Mom's to stay. She was always my landing pad when I came out of rehab or jail. I got settled back in and waited for her to leave for work in the morning. As soon as she was gone, I went into the backyard and looked for my ride. My bike had been swallowed up by weeds since I'd been away. Actually, it was someone else's bike that I'd stolen from their yard just before I went to rehab. Back when I stole it, it had tires. It didn't have tires anymore. Those were punctured and worn away over the countless hours on my circuit between scams and buys. After riding on flat tires for a while, they simply fell off. I didn't replace the tires because money wasn't for tires. Money was for heroin. I rode that bike on metal wheels to my dealer's house. Like my bike wasn't my bike, his house wasn't his house. It was the trap house he was selling out of.[20]

I was anxious. I didn't want to wait another second. "Can I shoot up here?"

"No." My dealer didn't want it in his house.

"Come on, man…"

"You can use the shed out back."

I knew the risk. I knew my tolerance was down. The staff had warned me in rehab as I was getting out. I only cooked a quarter of my usual dose, just to play it safe.[21]

---

[20] A trap house is an abandoned home or building dealers use as a storefront. They used to be called "shooting galleries" back in the day.
[21] Now, rehabs will send people home with Narcan. It's a good thing they do. Narcan is a drug that counteracts opiates. It is a life-saving drug for someone who is OD'ing.

Then I woke up. It was night time. 14 hours had passed. And somehow, I wasn't in the shed anymore. I was in an alley and I was soaking wet.

It wasn't hard to deduce what happened. If a dealer sells dope and the dope kills a customer, that's an involuntary manslaughter charge. Dealers do *not* want dead addicts in their backyard. The dealer must have found me OD'd in the shed and moved me to die somewhere else. He probably had some help, and I guess they splashed water on me hoping it would wake me up.

I got up and got my bearings. I was on Palmer, off Lagrange. If you are from Toledo, you know exactly where I'm talking about, and you know why it is not a neighborhood you want to wake up in.

***

Back To My Date With Monica

Monica comes from a good family. She's never done drugs before. She's never experienced addiction or witnessed it up close before. She had no idea about the world I came from. We'd only been seeing each other for about three months, and she just learned at that moment who she was really spending time with. But getting to know each other is what dating is for, right?

I was in the bathroom for about 20 minutes. The longer I was in there, the more she wondered what the hell was going on. She knocked on the door. No answer. She called my name. "Matt? Everything okay?" No answer. She pushed the door, but something was blocking it. Peeking through the gap, the obstacle was my limp, unconscious body. Then she saw my kit resting on the sink. Needle and spoon. She hadn't been around this life before, but no one's so sheltered that they wouldn't understand what was going on. She also saw my gun. Did I forget to mention the gun? We'll come back to that later…

Monica should have bailed. But she was different. My intuition at Bier Stube was right. Monica is special.

I don't know how she did it, but she was able to get her arm through the gap and lift me with one arm, just enough to open it. She called 911 as my ragdoll body was propped between the wall and the bathtub. She kept it pretty cool, all things considered. She did chest compressions and CPR on me.

Once the 911 operator assured her that help was on its way, she also had the forethought to hide my drugs and gun before emergency services arrived. Maybe some latent Italian genes suddenly expressed, because she slipped right into the role of the mafioso's woman. Even in that fucked up moment, adrenaline pumping, she set aside panic and was thinking about how to protect me.

The medics arrived and managed to fit into that tiny bathroom. They Narcan'd me and performed chest compressions, but I didn't regain consciousness. Monica watched all this happen. I know it was traumatic for her. I threw her into the deep end of the pool, but the way she handled it still impresses the hell out of me.

If Monica hadn't come back and made me have dinner with her, I'd be dead. If I'd been just a little more patient and waited for Monica to leave, I'd be dead. If I'd been a little weaker at that moment, I'd be dead. If Monica hadn't known how to pick the lock, I'd be dead. There'd be no book. There'd be no more story. I'd be a heartbreaking memory for my mom, I'd be a sad story for Monica, I'd be a painful memory and irreplaceable absence for my son, and I'd be a paragraph in the Toledo Blade.

Monica saved my life.

***

Everyone knows fentanyl is strong. Most people have no idea just how strong it is.

Fentanyl is so strong, it's measured in micrograms, 1 *millionth* of a gram. A small mosquito weighs about 2.5 milligrams. Just *half* of 1 milligram will probably kill you, especially if you haven't been using regularly. Double that dose is near certain death, even for an addict. I don't know how much I took. If I wanted to pick a safe dose, I'd need to put it on a scale so sensitive that it could accurately weigh an eyelash. *That's* how strong fentanyl is. That's why you hear about it in the news every week. That's why it seems like everyone knows someone who knows someone who died of fentanyl poisoning.

I woke up in the ICU. The first time I OD'd, I lost 14 hours. This time, a nurse told me I'd been there for three *days*. I was intubated and put on a ventilator. My vitals were declining, and they weren't getting any response from me. I lost blood to my brain for a while. They gave me a 10% chance of living. They told Monica and my mom to come up and say their goodbyes to my unconscious body. I have photos of my friends hugging me, believing this was our last moment together. It's a wild thing to look at. Most people never get to see the photos taken at their own wake.

I was a goner. But then things got better. I started breathing on my own. I woke up.

Call it luck. You can call it a miracle if you like. Call it divine intervention. Destiny. I don't know what to call it. I'll say this, though: there were a hundred things that could have gone differently that day. If even one thing had been different, I'd be dead. There are a hundred timelines where I don't live, and somehow, I got the one winning ticket. Once again, I got one more chance that I didn't deserve.

Someone left me their card while I was intubated in the hospital. The DART unit. Drug Abuse Response Team. I'd heard about them before, but I never gave them much thought. They were plainclothes police working for the Sheriff's Department who visited ODs in the hospital and offered to help them out. I was unconscious and dying when they came, but one of them left a card for me on the end table in the hospital room while I was unconscious. Strange that they did that, seeing as how the doctors thought I was definitely going to die. I guess the officer had a little hope for me. Somehow, their card ended up in my wallet. I don't know if they put it there, or if I did. My memory of that time is pretty fuzzy.

They told me something at an AA meeting. You can't keep it unless you give it away. Meaning, you can't stay sober unless you help others. Addiction is a disease of selfishness. You take from others. The only way out was to be selfless, to help others. I don't know why, but that stuck in my head, like that card stuck in my wallet.

***

They released me from the hospital with a new lease on life. A new chance. I had a son who almost lost his dad. I had a woman who cared for me, and who saved my life. I had a mom who never ran out of chances to give me. This was it. This is what I was saved for. This was the moment for me to get serious about sobriety. This was my moment to really do the work of confronting my addiction. This was the moment for me to go to rehab. I mean *really* go to rehab. It was time to get right with everyone: my family and friends, the people I'd hurt and betrayed and disappointed. It was time to get right with God and get right with myself.

I didn't, though.

Monica thought for sure there was no way Matt was ever going to fuck with drugs again. No way. Not after that. She'd be right if I wasn't an addict. She didn't know yet how addicts are.

I got high again the very next day.

Chapter 21: The Two Worst Things I Ever Did

Someone once asked me, "What's the worst thing you ever did to another person?"

I robbed someone at knifepoint. The first and only time I did that, I was desperate. I had nothing. No car. Mom was pissed at me and wasn't letting me in the house. Violence was never my thing. I was never a strong-arm robbery guy. I was about white-collar scams and scrap metal theft.

I came up to a lady at the ATM and put a knife to her back, just enough that she could feel it and know that I wasn't lying.

She turned around and looked me up and down. She didn't panic. I doubt her heart rate increased even 1 beat per minute. It's like that in high-crime neighborhoods. People become so used to it, that they learn to live with it. They get accustomed to hearing gunshots and sirens every night. They get used to young men looking at you like tigers deciding if you're an easy meal. People can get used to anything. When people live that way long enough, they develop a sixth sense, too. They can tune in on a frequency other people can't. They get really good at sensing who is dangerous and who is full of shit. She figured out who I was in about two seconds.

She laughed. "Get the fuck out of here." Then she turned back around and continued her business at the ATM.

She was right. I didn't stab her in the back. I ran away.

I hated myself for doing that. I hated myself while I did it. I still hate myself for that. I hated myself for even trying it when I couldn't go through with it. The sins that are hardest to forgive are your own. That one scares me. It scares me that I could be that person for even two minutes.

I owe that woman an apology, but even more than that, I owe her a thank you. That story could have ended with me doing hard time. Instead, she left me with an embarrassing story to share with you and the knowledge that I'll never have a future career in armed robbery.

The other one was making a pickup with my son in the car. I have to pause while writing about this. It makes me sick. Absolutely sick. Jackson was a little guy, maybe a year old. We roll up to this dealer, and Jackson was in the back strapped into a car seat. I give my dealer the money and he gives me the bag of dope, he sees Jackson and gets a big smile. "Hiiii." Waving at him, playing peek-a-boo with him. Under other circumstances, that'd be perfectly normal and wholesome. Jackson is looking at him, smiling, reaching out. My son and my dealer were playing like this was okay. Jackson waved back. Pure innocence, totally oblivious that the man on the other side of the car window was not a good guy. But at the same time, the guy who drove Jackson to him wasn't a good guy either.

That wasn't the first time I brought Jackson to a drug deal drive-thru, but that's the one I remember. I drove home sobbing the entire way. This was exactly the kind of shit Jackson's mom was protecting him from. This is exactly why she didn't trust me with him, why I didn't *deserve* him.

Jackson, I know someday you're going to read this part. The first story is embarrassing to tell, but this one is one of the hardest things for me to write. Drugs screw up your priorities. You were too little to leave home alone and I was feeling the sickness coming on. I've done so much regrettable shit in my life, but exposing you to that, even for just 5 minutes, is the worst thing I've ever done. If that's something that is hard for you to forgive me for, believe me when I say, forgiving myself is so much harder.

Now, when I look at a beer, I think about that. If drinking 1 beer makes me even 1% less of the good father I should be, it's not worth it.

I think it's every parent's hope to teach their kids how to not repeat their mistakes.

Chapter 22: Monica Is Kind Of Crazy

I got the gun because of some shit I got into with some FSU guys. I don't mean Florida State University students. These guys were a club called Friends Stand United (FSU), but they weren't Quakers. They're a straight-edge, anti-Nazi hardcore punk gang. They might not call themselves a gang, but at the time, that's how the FBI looked at them.

I don't remember exactly how it started–all the alcohol has made this period fuzzy–but I am not blameless. I definitely talked some shit to them in person and online. They pissed me off. Maybe because they were anti-drug or because they were flexing like they were tough guys. Whatever it was, we didn't get along. I busted their balls. They started threatening me. Alcohol and cocaine have a way of escalating situations. Me and my tattoo artist busted up one of their generals or leaders or whatever. It didn't seem like a big deal to us, but FSU took it seriously. Other chapters from other states got involved… and it became this whole thing.

The weird thing about cocaine is that it makes you feel invulnerable and paranoid at the same time. I wasn't in my right mind at the time, and it's hard to say now how much of it was in my head and how much of it was real.

So I carried a gun. Stupid. Very stupid.

Monica got rid of my gun when I overdosed. Thank you, Monica, because a gun was the last thing I needed in my life.

Here's how stupid I was. I went to bars, got brave from booze, and did cocaine until I felt like I was bullet-proof. Then I'd pick fights with strangers for no good reason. And I kept a gun for self-defense. Here I am, starting conflicts, putting myself and strangers in danger for nothing, just so I could feel like a tough guy, and I had a gun for my own safety. Drawing a loaded pistol in a fight *that I initiated* could not ever possibly improve the situation. It was stupid. Good riddance.

***

Monica is wise. By that I mean she knows what people should know about things that matter the most. I said she comes from money. Monica is the heiress of Marco's Pizza, one of the largest pizza chains on earth, a company with 1200 stores worldwide. She knows how to live in the public eye. She understands that perception is reality. She understands how to conduct herself. She knows how to choose her fights. She knows when to let things go.

She knows when to pump the brakes. If I want to buy a flashy car, she tells me to knock it off. If I see a cool watch, she reminds me I don't need a fancy watch. She reminds me that I don't need to impress people with objects. She reminds me that I don't even *really* want the watch. And she's right. She's got that old-money mentality. Don't flaunt. Don't be flashy. Don't waste it. Money is for building your future, it's not for toys and glamor.

When I was clean and pulling it together, I wanted to splurge a little. When you've been homeless, get clean, and finally have a little cash in your pocket, there's a temptation to indulge. She reminded me why it's stupid. She taught me a lot.

Monica knew about the civilized world out there. When it came to the streets and addiction, Monica started out in kindergarten. I helped her earn a PhD.

After that OD nearly killed me, Monica still stuck with me. I went to treatment, like I'd done and failed several dozen times before. I told her all the promises addicts tell. She believed them. She was still new to this.

While I was in treatment, I told her that I needed a change in my environment. I told her that when I got out of treatment, I needed my room to change. It was some addict logic that I came up with to get out of treatment early. As if there was some fentanyl feng shui that would cure me. It was nonsense.

When I came home, she had completely rearranged my place. She was so sweet. She really wanted to help. But she hadn't learned yet that addicts always lie.

***

One day I got a call from Monica.

"Hey."

"Look out the window."

I peeled back the curtains. She was outside the apartment, on the sidewalk. She had a box of my clean syringes that I was hiding in the Q-Tip. She had a dozen of them in her fist, caps off. She slammed them onto the side of the brick garage and dragged them, scraping off the tips. When the needles were totally fucked, she threw them and walked away.

It wasn't enough to just call me on it. She made me watch her destroy them. Monica's got some gangster in her.

***

I couldn't keep my place. I had to move back in with mom. Again.

"How do you get kicked out of your apartment? How do you have no money?" Monica asked me. It was a valid question.

I'd told her a month earlier that I only spent $5 a day on drugs. This time I told her the truth. I spent $100-200 a day. If I could only make $40 that day, it was *just* enough to get by but I would still feel sick. I had money for drugs but not for rent.

She slapped the shit out of me so hard I nearly fell off the porch stoop. She did not hold back. Then she just walked away and got in her car without anything else to say to me.

That's why addicts always lie.

But Monica kept coming back. I don't know why, but she believed in me. I know her friends and family were telling her to stay as far from me as possible. She loved me. She was loyal. She knew she could do better, but she loved *me*. Why?

I'd be honest with her sometimes. Honest in a way that's especially hard for a using addict. I'd come right out and say it. "I gotta go get high. I need to or I'm going to do something stupid."

She'd try to talk me out of it. She'd tell me why I shouldn't. Everything she said was right, but addiction is very persuasive. Eventually, I'd say, "I'm going one way or another. If it means that much to you, then come with me." I didn't think she'd take me up on the offer. After watching me nearly die on the worst date ever, she was terrified for me all the time. She wasn't about to let me OD again. Not without a chaperone.

She'd ride with me to whichever house I was buying from. She didn't come inside. I walked in, traded some bills for dope, and came right back out. We'd drive to a safe spot and pull over and she'd watch me get high. It was the best way she knew how to make sure I was safe. It made her feel better, but she died inside just a little. I hated seeing that.

I remember one time at one of these deals… it's one of those stories that's funny in hindsight, but at the time, it was very scary. I was meeting a dealer. He was flashy. He was the kind of dealer who was proud of what he did. He rolled up in a luxury SUV with spinner rims that cost at least five grand. Everything he wore looked like he bought it that morning. Uncomfortably heavy amounts of gold around his neck, wrists, and fingers. Just imagine if you dressed up as a caricature of a drug dealer for a Halloween costume party. You'd look exactly the same.

That was the first time Monica saw a guy I was buying from.

"You're giving him all this money? You're paying for all his chains and gold! Nah, fuck this piece of shit!"

Monica got out of the car before I even knew what to say back. I asked, "What're you doing?"

Monica, a young heiress with her nice clothes and expensive handbag, squared up to my drug dealer, finger in his face, "You know, you're a really mean guy! You're a piece of shit! People like you should be in prison."

"Monica, shut the fuck up!" I tried to get her back into the car. I was worried she was going to fuck up my relationship with the guy and he wouldn't sell to me anymore. I *should* have been worried about her life. She was yelling in my dealer's face, threatening him with prison. This was a guy who definitely had a heater strapped, in a neighborhood with so much crime the cops couldn't keep up.

To be fair, she was right. He *was* a piece of shit, even by drug dealer standards.

Lucky for both of us, he thought it was funny. He just laughed at her. That pissed her off more, which made it funnier for him. When the joke was getting old, he got back into his SUV, did a U-turn, and drove away. Monica wasn't done with him yet. She chased after him down Detroit and Delaware. On foot. Not on foot, on *heels*, talking shit the whole time. She couldn't stand that a guy like that was making money by slowly killing me.

And like I said. Monica's got some gangster in her.

Chapter 23: Mom Does The Right Thing

After that OD that nearly killed me, I have no memory of the next two months. It's almost a total blank. Something about the oxygen loss in my brain had some lasting effects. I do know a few things that happened during that blackout. I was fired from my job. Not because I missed those few days of work. They caught me stealing. I got a felony for that. I ran out of money and I lost the place I was renting. I was back with my mom on the East Side, again.

After all that, I know Monica was asking herself, "Why am I chasing this guy? He's on the East Side. He doesn't have a job. He's a felon. He lives with his mom. He's a drug addict. He seemed cool when I met him, but he is completely fucking up."

I wasn't getting better, and as she was realizing that, she wasn't so interested in spending time with me. How could she? She stopped coming around. She'd call me from time to time, just to check in. Maybe once a month, just to make sure I was still alive. Then she'd cry. I don't know if we'd ever said the words to each other yet, but she loved me. She loved me a lot. We weren't together, but she never moved on after me. She never committed to another guy. She was still loyal to me from a distance, like the loyal wife of a soldier on tour. She calls me. I'm still alive. Tears. Ok. Good. I'll talk to you later.

And my mom. My poor mom.

My mom put up with so much. So much. She didn't want to live in that house on the east side after the divorce, but that's what she could afford at the time. It was my fault. It was supposed to be temporary. Me and my addiction kept her there. I put my mom into debt almost immediately. This whole time, she was paying for my rehabs, my rent, my phone, my truck note, my bail, and my books in jail so I could buy from the commissary.

She took out a home equity line and borrowed against it. She couldn't pay her taxes and they put a lien on her house. She took out credit cards and kept maxing those out to keep buying me out of trouble. When she got behind, those debts went to collections. I nearly made her as homeless as I was.

The neighborhood had completely fallen apart. When she bought that house, it was worth maybe $60,000. A couple years ago, it was worth $40,000. Altogether, the money she owed on her mortgage, HELOC, tax lien, and cards came to about $80,000. My mom did that for me, to help me the best way she knew how. She was stuck in that neighborhood because of me.

It's not safe over there. I'm subscribed to crime alerts on my phone that will text me anytime there is a police call. There are drive-bys on her street all the time.

When people use the expression "victims of drug abuse," they usually mean the person abusing the drugs. They don't mean the people who are being abused by the addict. We *should*. I know I did that much damage to my mom because I've seen the bill. How much had I done altogether, counting everyone else I'd cheated, conned, or robbed for dope money? The city had hundreds of other people doing the exact same. The downstream effects of drugs are incalculable.

What I didn't know at the time was that my sister was talking to Mom, begging her to cut me off. I know it was murder for her to have to watch all that. She was telling my mom to knock it off, stop helping me, stop getting deeper into the hole for me. My sister was right. My mom was getting good advice she just wouldn't take.

It's funny. When we were kids, my sister was the rebellious one. I was the one who always did what he was supposed to.

It was 2015. I'd been doing this to her for nine years. I thought my mom would never quit on me. I was wrong about that. I found her limit. I pushed her all the way.

Having a loved one with a serious addiction is kind of like seeing them get cancer. First, you get the bad news. The doctor says it's treatable, but it's going to be a fight. Everyone is scared, but optimistic. The sickness gets worse. People become morose. In quiet, private moments, people wonder if this is it. What if this is the end? But then it gets better! The cancer is in remission! Things are looking up. But then it's back. It spread to somewhere else. It needs surgery. It's up and down like a rollercoaster. It metastasizes. Then it's in remission. Then there's a spooky dark spot on an x-ray. But it's benign. It can go on like that for years. It's dark. It's spiritually exhausting.

Addiction is kind of like that. It's an endless loop of hope and disappointment, forgiveness and betrayal. Eventually, people can't take it anymore. Everyone has a limit. Even moms.

I know it wasn't easy for her, but Mom finally kicked me out for real. I was back on the streets. I didn't really leave though. Every day, as soon as my mom left for work, I broke into her house. I could get in and out without doing any damage or leaving any trace. I could steal a snack, take a shower, hang out, and get high within that eight-hour window until she came back.

That was the third time I OD'd.

I was using in the kitchen and lost consciousness. I woke up on her kitchen floor, five hours later, my cheek against the linoleum floor, in a puddle of vomit. One little speck more, just a couple more micrograms, and my mom would have come back from a hard day at work and found her dead son on her kitchen floor.

I wonder if I went out like that… what would it have done to her? Would she blame herself? Would she be stuck with the crushing guilt of it, believing she killed me by kicking me out? Maybe she'd think it was a suicide, that I killed myself on purpose just to punish her, knowing she would find the body. Those questions without answers will haunt the survivors. I've known families who moved out of their homes because they couldn't bear the sight of the room where they found their loved one's body.

***

When Monica learned I was on the streets, she went looking for me. It's kind of funny in hindsight, but remember that she comes from a good family, and her only experience with addiction came from TV and movies. So when she went looking for me, she looked inside the dumpsters. She figured that's where I would be if I died. This put-together girl spent a few hours every week driving around the hood of east Toledo, looking inside dumpsters for my body. She had nightmares about it.

When we spoke on the phone, I'd tell her I was going to detox, going to rehab, just more bullshit to please her. The phone at detox was a blocked number. I'd go to the intake and call her from there, then leave against medical advice, and call her from a different blocked number. I'd be on the phone with her, telling her I was finally getting it together. I would tell her those lies while I was high as a kite in an abandoned, half collapsed building I was squatting in.

Monica was the one person I never stole from. Monica had money. She had purses. She carried cash. She would have been the easiest mark. Taking from her would have been so easy, and she had plenty to take. But even in my worst moments, I *never* stole from her. I took away her peace, her happiness, and many good nights sleep.

***

I was on the streets again. I was homeless many times, but usually not for very long. Eventually I'd always head back home to Mom.

In Northwest Ohio, summers are hot and muggy. The kind of weather where you have to peel your shirt off your body after an hour of yard work. The winters are just as harsh. On cold nights, the air will pull the heat out of you in a minute outside and it takes an hour to warm back up when you get back inside.

I went to food pantries to eat. Free food meant more money for dope. The food wasn't usually too bad, either. A lot of restaurants would donate the stuff they were throwing out anyway. I'm not too good for a day-old croissant from Panera.

But I never went to a shelter. Never. It's not that I was never cold, or I always had a soft place to lay my head. Maybe it was stubbornness. Maybe going to a shelter would be admitting that I was really homeless. Just like I wasn't like those other addicts when I was in detox, I wasn't like those other guys on the street. I could tell myself I wasn't *homeless* homeless. I could crash in my mom's garage, if I wanted to, or her van. I had a sleeping bag and usually had a whole abandoned house to myself. And the shelter was miles away from where I bought my heroin, so it was a hassle.

But most of all, I think I was afraid of them. They reminded me of jail.

I slept in abandoned buildings most nights. There wasn't any heat, but it kept the wind off me. I was in my mom's neighborhood a lot. One place I often squatted was down the alley on the other side of the block from my mom's house. I'd look through the glassless windows that kids had busted out with rocks and I could see the glow inside mom's house. Sometimes, when I saw her lights go out for bed, I'd sneak through the alley and into Mom's backyard. My mom had a busted-down minivan back there that she never used, never planned on fixing, and never bothered towing. It wasn't locked. I climbed in, quietly shut the door so she wouldn't hear, and I slept there. I just wanted to be close to her.

I love my mom. I know I had a lot of good things to say about my dad, but I'm a mama's boy. She never knew I was there. I wasn't even allowed on her property.

About six in the morning, just before the sun was up but the dope-sickness had just begun, I'd hear the creak of the rear screen door. It was Mom letting the dogs out. I could peek and see her for that brief moment. I had nothing but that pull inside me that ordered me up to get to work like a drill sergeant. All I wanted in those moments was to see my mom. Just to talk to her for a second. Just to hug her. I cried in that broken-down van.

Then one night, the van wasn't there. She'd finally gotten rid of it. It was a really cold October, dipping below freezing most nights. I needed to be somewhere and I was so homesick.

I walked onto her porch. I knocked on her door. The porch light came on. She opened the door, but she left the screen door between us closed. She didn't unlatch it. I could feel a little bit of the warmth from inside her home.

"What do you want, Matt?"

"Mom… I'm gonna freeze tonight. I was just hoping that maybe tonight I could sleep in your garage. Maybe a blanket. Maybe a space heater. I won't even come in. I just… I don't wanna die." That was true. It was cold enough that it could kill me. "I'm gonna go to rehab in a couple days." That wasn't true, though.

Something was different with her. She'd always give me food. She'd always let me stay there or shower. She always did something. She's my mom. She had to. Every time I came to her with a sob story, I could always get her to crack, just a little.

She took a deep breath and looked up. I could see she was trying to remember something. Something she'd rehearsed. "Matt, you'll always be my son but you are no longer my child. If you don't get off my porch, I'm calling the police."

She'd been learning. I didn't know how, but she was definitely learning about addiction, and talking with other people. They'd taught her to say that. She looked at me for a moment, seeing how I would respond. The look on my face probably said, "Where the fuck did that come from? I was not expecting that." I didn't say anything. I didn't know what to say. She didn't know what to say either. She shut the door slowly, then flicked the porch light back off.

I was stunned. I knew those weren't her words. I found out later that she was in some self-help groups, getting advice from other parents with kids with drug abuse problems. I also didn't know that as soon as she closed the door, she put her back to it, slid down, and sat there sobbing. Those weren't her words, and they were the hardest words she ever had to say. She knew I was lying about treatment. But she knew I wasn't lying about freezing. She knew those might be the last words she'd ever say to her son. She wasn't that hard. She was coached. But the second I was out of sight, she cried for hours on her living room floor.

***

AA talks about rock bottom. That's the point where you are so low, you can't go any lower. If you are one of my recovering addict readers, you know what I mean. If you are one of my non-addict readers, you don't. You think you do, but you don't. Whatever you think your rock-bottom is— whatever you think is the absolute worst you can make things for yourself—believe me when I tell you this: it can get so much worse. Rock bottom is miles lower than you think it can be.

That's why we sometimes call non-addict people "Earth people." We come from a different planet. We're like space aliens in a science fiction story. You have an idea about where we came from, but we lived it. While you were at the grocery store silently debating which of the 40 different types of individually sliced cheeses to purchase for a sandwich, people like me were behind that grocery store, breaking into one of the cashier's cars, and stealing a $70 pink iPod shuffle we prayed we could pawn for $5.

Monica was barely talking to me. A smart, beautiful, loyal woman who wanted me to be healthy, happy, and free. I pushed her away. I didn't cheat on her, but I may as well have. It was like I had two girls fighting for my attention and Miss Fentanyl won. I traded a good woman who loved me for a needle that was slowly murdering me every day.

I had no friends. I'd burned and used the real friends I had. The people I had fun with at Bier Stube wouldn't call me the life of the party anymore.

I'd trashed my inheritance. Thrown away a scholarship. Thrown away a real chance at a career playing ball. That was so long ago, I couldn't even remember the last time I'd watched a game on TV. I ruined a family. I built a business from nothing. I ruined that, too. What did my mom say? You'll always be my son but you are no longer my child. Jackson could have said something similar to me, because I had a son, but I wasn't being a father. Playing ball all those years ago was the most important thing in the world to me before I took that first pill. Now, I'd be happy to just throw a ball with my kid in the yard.

My mom's performance was perfect. I totally believed it. I believed that I'd fucked up so bad that my mom—a woman who'd always been there, always been everything a mom should be—no longer cared if I lived or died. That's how much of a piece of shit I was. I wasn't even good enough to sleep in her garage.

That was my rock bottom. I wanted to stand out. I wanted to fit in. I wanted friends. I love people and I want them to love me. This was the exact opposite of that. This was the perfect opposite of happiness and goodness. This was Hell. I'd tried rehab a few dozen times and I was convinced that didn't work.[22] There was no way out. No way out. The thing about Hell is, it's forever.

***

The next day, I had a mission. I knew a guy named Tim that I would get high with sometimes. He'd let me stay the night once in a while when I needed a place to crash. You could almost call him a friend, but I didn't really have any of those anymore. He'd go to the food pantry on Sunday mornings.

Mom told me to get off her porch on Saturday. The next morning, Tim wasn't home. I broke into his apartment. I knew where he kept his gun. He'd shown it to me before. A pistol.

I left with it inside my waistband.

---

[22] The keyword is "work." It's work and I never did the work. But I didn't know that yet.

Chapter 24: People Who Died

While I was using, I knew probably about 100 people who died. Maybe more.

In 2021, 5,585 Ohio residents died from an overdose.[23] I don't mean there were 5,585 trips to the ER for overdose. I mean *died* of an overdose. In 1999, long before I had my first sip of beer, that number was 327. Read that again if you have to. I sure did.

Less than 1 body a day to almost 15 bodies *a day*. Put that number against anything that scares the hell out of people. Put those numbers up against every serial killer in American history *combined*.

More Ohioans die of an overdose every year than the number of Americans that died in the entire Iraq war.[24] I keep hearing about this war on drugs. We must be losing it because we're fighting it on our home soil and the casualty reports are horrifying.

***

I've seen a lot of death. My dad's death was the hardest.

The second hardest death was the only time I've ever watched someone die. I didn't really know her. It happened while I was in a lockdown psychiatric ward. She'd snuck some drugs in. That wasn't unusual.

I was half asleep in my room when I heard people shouting "Code red! Code red!" I opened the door and right in front of me,

---

[23] Ohio sees 26 percent increase in fatal drug overdoses | wkyc.com
https://www.wkyc.com/article/news/local/ohio/deadly-drug-overdoses-ohio-statewide-data-2021/95-d7582aa9-b835-49d6-9868-1c7036de890a

[24] https://www.businessinsider.com/how-many-people-have-been-killed-in-iraq-and-afghanistan#6951-us-military-deaths-1

staff were performing chest compressions on a woman. Her shirt was torn open and they'd already applied AED sticky pads. I'd never seen CPR performed before, except on dummies or in movies. It was violent. They pressed so hard, that I expected to hear her ribs crack. I didn't know it then, but that's something that actually happens a lot. When the man pressed down on her, I could see her belly inflate. They told me to get back into my room and shut the door. I did. Just feet away, a woman was dying. And here I was, pretending not to hear the panicked people on the other side after this woman handed them the terrible responsibility of saving her life.

I looked out the window. There were colorful bursts in the sky and distant pops. I didn't realize what day it was. It was the 4th of July. My favorite holiday. I watched someone die on my favorite holiday.

I left rehab the next day. The first thing I did was get high.

***

In jail, no one helps you out. And if they do, they do it secretly. It's different on the streets. Addicts don't have friends, except other addicts. And the only thing they have in common is their common interests. You see the same people around at the food pantry, at the clinic, at a meeting, at a flophouse, at a dealer's house. In a fucked up way, they are like colleagues. Your job, your career, is getting high, and so is theirs. Sometimes, you're even coworkers. It's a shitty job and no one knows it better than we do. So we try to give each other a hand until one of us inevitably stabs the other in the back.

Older addicts will take on apprentices, younger people who are new to it, to teach them the way of the needle. Drug mentorship is common. This type of coaching comes from people who survived long enough that the only thing they have is good advice for bad behavior.

I taught a young guy to shoot. He was crushing pills and snorting them, or snorting heroin.

"Man, what are you doing?" This youngster isn't getting everything out of it. He's basically wasting perfectly good dope that way. "Lemme show you how to shoot it." He thanked me for the good advice.

He was an apt pupil. He died a week later.

That one weighed on me for a long time. Did I play a part in that? It took me a long time to get past that. If he didn't learn it from me, he would have learned it from someone else. Maybe from YouTube, like I did.

***

How could an anti-drug PSA on TV talk me out of it? How could jail? *Death itself* didn't motivate me to quit. A hundred dead or more weren't enough examples to make me stop. You get used to it. It's amazing what people can get used to. Sleeping in abandoned houses on cold Ohio nights. Hurting other people. Hurting yourself. I dealt with some seriously bad folks on a daily basis, dodging cops and people I'd ripped off. Every day a new pair of eyes were out there on the streets attached to someone who had a good reason to fuck me up. Every day, losing friends and making enemies. You can get used to anything.

I still hear the names of people I used to know. For the last eight years of being sober, I've heard the name of someone who just passed almost every day. Someone I used to know. Even now that I'm clean, the names keep coming. Many were acquaintances. Some were friends. But two names found me in 2022, and they hit me hard. Sam and Bryce. We were close back in the bad old days. We were also close in the good old days, the sober days. I hear names all the time, but hearing Sam and Bryce broke my heart.

All I can do is keep their memory to keep me sober. They wouldn't want me to follow after them. Now, death is my strongest motivator. For most people, you can take a doctor-prescribed pill or have a beer on a Friday night and be fine. Not me. For me, it's a death sentence.

Chapter 25: The Card

So I had Tim's gun. I had a mission. One last hurrah. I was gonna steal some shit, get some dope, then I was going back to mom's house.

Mom was at work. I went into the garage. I set up a chair to sit on. I cooked, tied, and pushed the last dope I had. I set out the kit in front of me like I was staging a crime scene. I loaded the gun and chambered a round.

If I can't live in the garage, then I'll die in the garage.

I put it in my mouth.

You never forget the taste of a loaded gun. The taste of metal. The bitter flavor of gunpowder residue from every round that passed through that barrel. You can taste the lubricant on the slide. You never forget that taste.

My finger was on the trigger.

I pictured how it would go after I was gone. My mom would come home from work. I imagined her walking a little slower than she did in the morning, her feet sore from being on them all day waitressing. I pictured my mom, busting her ass, serving people. Scrambling between tables and hoping the tips were generous. I thought of my mom coming home from work, ready to just turn in and go to sleep. Instead, she finds her baby boy in her garage, the back of his head opened up like a bowl full of bolognese.[25]

Then I thought about how fucking unfair that was for her. What a dickhead move. Nine years and I hadn't already put her

---

[25] That's meat marinara, in case you don't know Italian food. It's really good, so I hope I didn't ruin it for you.

through enough? She cleans up for people every day, and now I'm gonna make her clean up the inside of her child's head in her garage? Why? Why should she? Because I fucked up? Because I made all the wrong choices? If someone else did that to her, I'd hate them for it.

I broke down. I took the gun out of my mouth. Screaming. Sobbing. The kind of cry you only do when you're born and when someone you love dies. The kind of cry you only do a few times in your life.

I scared the shit out of myself. This was one of those moments of clarity, when the high finally gives you a chance to think. What the *fuck* am I doing? I used to *love* life. I realized that I still did. There is so much beauty in this world. Seconds earlier, I was just five pounds of pressure away from ending it. Five pounds is nothing. If I have a big meal, I can weigh myself in the morning and be five pounds heavier. That's how close I was. *Fuck.* I had never thought about doing something like that before. Never in my life.

Fuck. I almost did to Jackson what my dad's cancer did to me.

No. It's not even close. This would've been so much worse.

Fuck!

Rehab doesn't work. I can't keep using. I can't keep being homeless. I can't keep doing this and hurting everyone I love. What can I do?

"I gotta go to jail."

I had three felony warrants: One in Michigan for the home invasion of the detective's house, one in Pennsylvania for robbing Dawn's family, and one in Ohio for stealing from my employer. I was already a felon. I wasn't allowed to own a gun. Add handling a firearm while on drugs, that's another charge.

Fuck it. Bring the cops.

I figured I'd go to prison for five years at least. Maybe more. That'll give me some time to stay sober and figure things out, maybe make amends. At least just give Mom, Monica, and Jackson a break from all the bullshit I've been putting them through. They'd know I was sober. They'd know where I was. They'd know how to reach me. Shit. Doing some time on the 4th floor would be a gift.

I don't know why I didn't call 911. Instead, I looked inside my wallet. No cash. No credit cards. Just an ID and that card the DART unit left with me while I was unconscious for three days.

***

What is DART?

> A brief aside: We have to talk about DART. The Drug Abuse Response Team was started by Sheriff Tharp in 2014 in Toledo. Back when that card was in my wallet, DART was still new. Since then, it's become a national movement.
>
> Sheriff Tharp understood that there was a drug war, and the drugs were winning. Cops saw it and lived it every day. DART had a different ideology. Incarceration didn't work. Addicts interact with the law all the time, and it makes sense to use that as an opportunity to intervene and get them into treatment. Right after an OD is the perfect time to stop in and offer help.
>
> The program started with just 2 officers and a grant from Governor DeWine. It grew into a team of about 20 officers. They started traveling to other departments all over the country to train them how to do it. DART is the name of this team, but they call the practice a Quick Response Team. Eight years later, quick-response teams are

everywhere. Almost every mid to large-sized county you go to has these.

The work they've done is tremendous. I don't know who put that card in my wallet while I was in the hospital, but that was the second time a cop saved my life.

Now back to your regularly scheduled autobiography.

***

I'd opened that wallet a hundred times and saw that card in there. Every time I saw it, I thought there was no way I was calling the cops on myself. At least once a day, I opened my wallet, saw the card, mentally said, "No thank you" to DART, took out my cash, closed my wallet, and paid my drug dealer. I did that *every day*. But I left the card in there.

I called DART. Hopefully, they'll arrest me.

They asked, "Are you going to kill yourself?"

"No. I can't. I already tried that."

"Can you find a way to make it through the next twelve hours?"

"Yeah."

"Okay. I'll come pick you up at seven in the morning."

"Yeah. Cool." Easiest arrest ever.

***

The next morning didn't go as I expected. He didn't put handcuffs on me, read me my rights, and ease my head under the doorway into the back of a Crown Vic. He picked me up like he was an Uber driver. He gave me a cigarette and let me smoke in his car. It was that time of year when the sky and concrete wore matching colors. The animals are all gone. No birds are singing, no crickets are chirping. You don't even see people outside, except when they're hustling between a parking spot and a door. That time of year, the only sounds in Toledo come from machines and wind that cuts through the leafless trees, carrying the cold off the Maumee River. Days like these can be bleak. Not today. Today was my lucky day. Today, I was going to jail.

Except I wasn't. My ride drove me to the Zepf Center. I must have gone there 12 times already. I'd been there six times just that year alone.

"This isn't jail. This is rehab. What're we doing, dude?" I asked. He must have heard the disappointment in my voice.

"What you did is not normal. People don't call the cops on themselves. You're sick and you need treatment."

This was a guy who got it. I didn't get it. Not yet. But *he* gets it. Most police would run my name and take me straight to jail. I just happened to be in the one place in America with this new kind of policing. If I had called the police on myself in any other city, I would be writing this book from prison.

Catholics have a saint for everything. Jude is the saint of lost causes. If ever there was a saint for me, Jude was my guy. People talk about angels watching over them, bringing those small miracles that change everything. I had an angel that day. I truly believe my dad sent that person to pick me up. Dad sent me someone who didn't care that I'd failed rehab 27 times. A total stranger who thought I was worth one more try.

Like I said. Catholics have a saint for everything. But my favorite is St. Roy.[26]

---

[26] I'm not blaspheming, I know my dad wasn't literally canonized. I'm just saying the man was the best ever.

Chapter 26: The 2015 Class Reunion

I'd detoxed at Zepf so many times, I couldn't even remember the number. This time was different. It was a bad detox. They all hurt like hell, but this one hurt worse.

You can pray to God to change your situation. Sometimes God wants the situation to change you.

When I came out of it, my head was different. For the first time, I felt lucky to be there. I was in Zepf instead of on the street. It's not a fancy place, but just being able to get up and get a cup of coffee anytime I liked felt like a gift. I'm not in a trap house. I'm not behind bars, in withdrawal, curled up into a ball on the cold, concrete cell floor, shaking and shitting my jumpsuit while my bunky tells me to shut the fuck up because he's trying to sleep. I could go to the bathroom and close the door. *Any time I wanted* I could do that. I could just go get a granola bar if I wanted one. It blew my mind. You'd think I escaped from North Korea and was visiting Boca Raton. I remember brushing my teeth and it felt so weird. I hadn't done it in so long, it was like an alien probe in my mouth. I'd been away from normal for so long, I didn't even understand it anymore.

"So this is what being an earth-person is like."

When I was on day two, I saw some other clients a couple days ahead of me, and how much better they were doing than I was. They could smile again. They even laughed sometimes. I saw a guy doing push-ups and I thought, "Oh, man. I miss push-ups. I want to do push-ups. I miss sports." It had been so long since I thought about sports. I looked forward to those push-ups. It motivated me. If I stuck it out for a few days, I might be well enough to do push-ups. The smallest shit felt like a miracle.

After the worst of it was over and I wasn't shitting myself and vomiting, I went to group therapy. We all knew each other from treatment, jail, or the streets. The regulars. The addiction alumni. I wasn't the only one there who was different. We'd all been through this so many times. We'd seen fentanyl wiping us out. There were always new faces, but some people we used to know faded away. They'd stop being around and one day you wonder, "Hey, I haven't seen so-and-so in a while. Where's he been?" And someone tells you he died five months ago.

I'd been in a lot of group therapy. A *lot*. I can't explain it, but *this* group was different from every other group I've been in. I've sat in a hundred circles, talking about the same things over stale coffee in small paper cups. Something had changed. Whatever it was that got into me was in them, too. They were motivated, too. It was another small miracle to add to my collection. If I'd been to that detox just a week earlier, those group sessions never would have happened. Things happened when they had to happen. Things lined up exactly how they needed to line up. It was those people, in that place, in those limited spots, at the same time. And more than that, we sat together when Toledo needed help more than ever.

***

October 17th is my *other* birthday. It's the day we decided we would hold ourselves—and each other—accountable. That was when we decided to go through the whole program together instead of leaving against medical advice. We agreed that we would all make it to the next step as a team. Let's be actual friends, not using friends. Not just people who get high together and stab each other in the back.

It was corny. It was so corny, it's almost embarrassing to type this out. We started a little club of people who wanted to stay away from drugs and try to be good and to do good. A club needs a name.

Someone said, "We're kind of like a team. We need a team name."

Someone else suggested, "We're in recovery. We're a team. So… let's call it Team Recovery."

We took that name literally. Before every group therapy session, we huddled together and put our hands in, "1… 2… 3… Team Recovery!" I didn't just miss sports. I missed this. I missed being on a team.

It was so fucking Hallmark and I loved it. Good things are corny, sometimes. Almost every Christmas movie is corny. People like corny. And we were being as corny as it gets. And it worked.

Team Recovery completed detox. All of us. No man left behind.

Detox is seven days. Treatment is something else. Treatment is where the real work begins.

We all went to the recovery house together. It's sober living with continued treatment. We weren't ordered by a court to be there, but we couldn't just go home. We couldn't go back to the way we were living, either. It's a home for addicts all working towards the same thing: one more day of sobriety. One more chance to break my all-time high score on staying sober.

You are who you surround yourself with. If you hang with dramatic people, your life will become dramatic. If you hang with criminals, sooner or later you'll be in it. Hang with mentally healthy, good people and you can't help but be like them. Going back to the streets was not an option.

We became those happy healthy people. We became the people we needed to surround ourselves with.

***

There were six of us. The Dirty Half-Dozen. In the movie *Ocean's 11*, everyone has their specialty. There's a computer hacker guy, a flexible acrobat guy, a smooth-talker, and a planner. Everyone has strengths. That's how it was with us.

That guy doing push-ups was the tough man of the group. There are "tough guys," guys who act tough because they want you to know they're tough. But then there are tough guys. Tough enough to do push-ups while anyone else would be crumpled up in bed. He gave me hope. An athletic guy, like I used to be, like I wanted to be again. He inspired me. He's the real deal. When we were mobbed with hate on social media, he didn't give a fuck. There's "I don't give a fuck," like how Eminem says it, where he's screaming it so you think maybe he actually does kind of give a fuck. This guy? He did not give an actual fuck! It's good to have guys like that in your corner.

One woman in the group was kind of like our secretary. She was quiet but observant and alert. She kept the minutes and kept us focused. If our group had a mom, it was her. She cried when things got emotional, as things often do during recovery. But she was always there for people when they weren't feeling it. Confrontation can be tough. Confronting yourself and others and holding each other accountable usually isn't easy.

We had a tough guy, but we also had a tough girl. She was from the Bronx and moved out to Toledo to be with her family. Tough undersells it, actually. She was bad. Dangerous. She was no fucking joke. She'd been arrested for trafficking weapons and she'd done hard time for it. She was hard-nosed, and wouldn't sugarcoat a single word out of her mouth. There's a certain kind of scary that only a woman can be.

We had a workhorse. The kind of guy any employer dreams of having. He would do whatever needed to be done when it needed doing. He's a guy who won't sit still. When you ask him to jump, he doesn't ask how high, he says he already jumped a half hour ago.

We had the man with the mission. Always lending an opinion based on some form of evidence-based research. Absolute Zen-like focus on the task. Always zeroed in. Always on point, and quick to notice when anyone needed steering. When people were distracted with other ideas and other projects, he was the man to set you straight.

Then there was me. I was the public relations and media guy. I knew computers the best because of my experience with the lawn business and (not) selling fake IDs. I could handle legal stuff, nonprofits, and relationship management. Maybe I'm giving myself too much credit, but if we were Ocean's 11, I was Ocean.

Others came and went, but these were the founding mothers and fathers.

***

We survived detox together, we would do recovery together, too. We made a list together of things we wanted to do. Things we couldn't do as using drug addicts. We made promises to ourselves and each other about what we could achieve, and what we could have if we stayed off the needle, pill, powder, or bottle.

We wanted to start a nonprofit. Wristbands. T-shirts. We wanted to organize community events. Speak to kids at school. Most importantly, we wanted to help other people find treatment. We wanted to share what we had with anyone who would have it.

We started working with DART, and oftentimes we were on-call to get to hospitals and talk to individuals who had overdosed, or to their families if they weren't conscious.

We made a game plan. We wrote it down. What was wrong with the system as it was? No one knew the system better than we did. What could we do differently?

1. **Treatment Navigation**

When Team Recovery met in rehab in 2015, there were 16 Medicaid detox beds in the entire county. Now there are about 200. In 2015, Narcan was a controversial medicine, and now it is everywhere.

It's harder to find treatment for addiction than it is to find a dentist who will take your insurance. Some places only take Medicaid. Some places only take private insurance. Some only take Medicare. Some only take people with no insurance. Some are only in-patient. Some are only out-patient. Some have methadone and suboxone, others don't. Some do detox, others don't.

If you're lucky enough to have insurance as an addict needing treatment, insurance will only cover you for some places, not others. Private insurance can be very specific about it. They might only cover you if you go to a free-standing facility that is accredited by the Joint Commission. If you have no idea what that means, don't worry. Nobody knows that shit. Imagine being a parent or spouse trying to get their loved one some help, but you can't get any until you navigate a labyrinth of bureaucracy. You don't know anything. You call around. You Google a lot of terms you don't know.

And many of them will click the first Google hit for "drug rehab near me." At the very top are the clinics that paid Google to go to the top of the rankings. Those places aren't always "near me." More often than not, they are all the way down in Southern Florida.

It can take days. It can take longer. Many people never figure it out. You don't have time for this. They need help now, but the process is so complicated.

This was causing problems for people. It caused problems for us while we were using. We wanted to fix that. The system is extremely complex but we knew the system. We've gone through it a dozen times or more. We can guide them through it. We can skip the whole learning process and get them to where they need to be ASAP. No one else was doing it. We had to do it.

2. **Prevention in Schools**

It's better to be proactive than reactive. It's better to get a diagnosis early before it becomes life-threatening.

No one was doing it because no one was paying for it. That's fine by us. We already took so much from society, we knew we were deep in the red. We were happy to pay it back. We don't need money to tell kids not to repeat our mistakes.

3. **Family Support**

We fucked up our families. We victimized them. We took them as emotional hostages. We seriously damaged their ability to trust.

Someone taught my mom how to say those words, "You'll always be my son but you are no longer my child. If you don't get off my porch, I'm calling the police." If someone had taught her that 9 years earlier, maybe I wouldn't have been on the streets as long as I was. Families need help. They need support. They need groups. Families need help like my mom needed help.

Those already exist, but many of them are very principle-driven. Certain topics are off-limits. There are rules about what you can and cannot say. Al-Anon (usually) prefers to have discussions about alcohol. We were trying to deal with a heroin epidemic. Some places are cool and will accept people. I've been told by other places, "We can only talk about alcohol here."

Some places are very strict with enforcing those kinds of rules, especially the old-timers. Others will let anyone in because they just want to see you get better. If you go to that first kind, it can be scary.

One of the first things we did when we got to the halfway house was make signs and stand on the corner of Cherry and Summit. Positive signs. Good vibes. We wanted to help break the stigma of addiction. It wasn't a lot, but we were just getting started. We took photos and posted them on our group's Facebook page.

Chapter 27: This Time, I Listen

At 90 days sober, I got a job making $25 an hour. I was so happy. I had never made money like that before. I had benefits. I could work overtime. When I wasn't at work, my free time was spent on *the* work, giving back. We went to schools and donated our time to help someone before they needed our help. People booked us for events. They called them "town halls" but they weren't usually at the town hall. We were invited to panel discussions. People were reaching out to us from all over, including Washington, DC.

You have to help others to help yourself. You can't keep it unless you give it away. That's what they told me in AA.

It's not optional. It's essential. When we help others, we help ourselves. Even in my previous attempts at recovery—even when I went to the meetings—I was taking from others. I was taking time. Taking good will. Taking burnt coffee and a styrofoam cup. Taking them seriously was the only thing I *didn't* take, the one thing they wanted me to have. It's so clear now, but I couldn't see it then.

Everything about recovery is about humbling yourself. I for sure wasn't ready to hear that. When I started, I told myself I wasn't like these other addicts. Matt is special. Matt is different. I could handle it this time. My ego was my greatest weakness. It always has been. You can't recover until you get outside of yourself. That's why AA famously includes a non-denominational Higher Power, God, Allah, Yahweh, the Tao, or maybe a vague spiritual power out there somewhere. As long as it is significant to you personally, the name doesn't matter. What matters is that you acknowledge that there are forces bigger than you.

I've heard many teachers say that they learn by teaching. Students ask questions. A lot of questions. Questions the teacher hadn't thought about or asked themselves. A teacher has to find an answer. Helping others find recovery is a lot like that. They help me as much as I help them.

***

I didn't understand the steps until I worked them with the help of a sponsor. I never asked anyone to explain them to me. Once I tried—I mean really tried, and finally understood what the steps were about—it blew my mind. The information isn't just good for addicts. It's good advice for anyone.

The Big Book was published in 1939. At that time, there were only four doctors who specialized in addiction in the whole country. Now there are at least four in every city. The book was a collaboration and included one of these rare specialty doctors. They struggled to develop a successful treatment model. Medicine didn't work.

The only thing that worked was alcoholics helping each other.

People with advanced degrees from prestigious colleges, experts in the human mind and behavior, none of them could figure it out. The simple solution was one alcoholic talking to another alcoholic.

I skipped the talking part. I didn't understand it because I didn't do it. I hadn't ever talked it through. Saying you're too busy to go to meetings is like saying you're too busy to stop for gas because you're driving. Maybe you don't need to go to the meeting that day, but someone at that meeting needs you. There were plenty of times I told myself, "I got this." I was wrong every time. Skipping meetings is just the first of many "I got this's" that I don't got.

***

I say my prayers and I meditate. I still do that every single day. I reflect on my mistakes. Even something little, I see it, I acknowledge it, and I consider how to fix it. Maybe I said something unkind to a coworker. Maybe I don't know if they took it badly or took it as a joke. Either way, I need to fix it. I can't have those things pile up. I can't have resentments accumulate. I cannot invite negativity into my life. When things get dark like that, I know what I do. I drink. And when I'm drunk, it's easy to say yes to cocaine. Then I hear heroin whispering to me again, asking me to take her back. You know the rest.

I won't go back. Not one inch closer to going back. They put flaps behind race horses' eyes, called "blinkers," so the horses can't see behind them. The riders and owners want the horse focused entirely on what's in front of them. That's true for horses, and it's also true for people. Where you're looking is where you're going.

***

Many people find their way to Christianity during recovery. Some are lapsed believers, and some grew up believing something else, or in nothing at all. There are a lot of religions in the world—and I'm no expert, so forgive me if I get this wrong—but I can't think of any religion that emphasizes forgiveness like Christianity does. When you are in recovery, you have a lot of things to ask forgiveness for. A lot of things you don't deserve forgiveness for. You can see the appeal of baptism, of washing away sins.

Today is your first day of being clean. Today is the first day of the rest of your life. Today you are born again, and this time you can do it the right way. You'll stumble. You'll fail. Because that's what humans are and that's what humans do. But you are forgiven. You're on the right path. Tell that bag of powder, "Get thee behind me, Satan!"

And there are lots of people who have done a lot worse than I have. Don't get it twisted, though. I'm not better than they are. The only reason I didn't do some of those things is because I never believed I had to. There are things I didn't do—and I'm so glad I didn't do—but I would have. If you put me in a situation where that was my only way, I would have.

"There but for the grace of God go I."

I've heard some real horror stories at meetings, and the monster in the story is usually the person telling it. I don't look down on them. I can't. Because I know that if things went a little differently, things got harder, things got a little scarier, a little more desperate, then it'd be me up there telling that story.

Chapter 28: Give It Away

While I was at the recovery house, I spent a lot of time studying addiction. I needed to know everything I could. It was just like when I was a kid obsessing about learning every vocabulary word. I'd read as much science as I could find. Psychology, psychiatry, biology, neurology, anything that could give me insight into what was going on with me and the people I was living with, the people we needed to help.

In the late 70s, Canadian psychologists at Simon Fraser University experimented with addiction in rats. The experiments are now fondly called Rat Park. In Rat Park, rats were given a choice: drink regular water or drink water with sweetened morphine in it. There were two groups. Some rats were placed in isolation, in small cages, with nothing to do. Other rats were put into a larger cage, among more rats, and the cage had the kinds of things that rats like: wheels to run on and tubes to climb through.

The groups in isolation got hooked on dope and killed themselves with morphine. The ones in the community didn't show any interest in getting high. None at all. Isolation from the community and from activity caused the rats to seek drugs, not the drugs themselves. The experiment has been repeated many times. They don't always end with a perfectly sober Rat Park, but they always produce a more sober Rat Park.

"Breaking stigma" isn't just a buzzword that looks good on copy. Breaking stigma doesn't mean "not hurting people's feelings." Stigma separates people. Separation from the community—separation from Human Park, if you will—drives people towards drug abuse, and makes it impossible to escape. Team Recovery only worked because we worked together. Our little group was enough community to get us to stop sipping off that morphine bottle and get back on the hamster wheel. (I realize I'm stretching this analogy to its breaking point, and I'm sorry for that.)

Stigma (especially criminal records) makes it hard for recovering addicts to get jobs. It makes it hard to rent a place to live. Stigma keeps people stuck. Recovering addicts can't connect with society if society won't connect with them. That's one reason why a community of addicts works, because none of us are in a position to judge each other.

***

In the spirit of breaking stigma, Team Recovery went out to a downtown intersection one day and held up signs. It was simple, and it was something many of us already had experience with when begging for change. In a way, we were still asking for change, but not the kind that jingles.

The signs were simple messages. The one people remember best was the perfect, simple message:

> FUCK HEROIN

The Team Recovery Facebook page had seven followers that morning. The next day we had *thousands*. Our post had gone super-viral. We couldn't believe what we were looking at. People were giving thumbs up and sharing it, over and over. A lot of what appears on the Facebook feed is pure negativity, bickering, politics… but our positivity was cutting right through it.

We started getting messages. A lot of messages. Not just "Good job" and "Love the sign." We were hearing from people who needed help, for themselves or from loved ones. People shared their stories with us, both terrible and familiar.

It was more than we knew how to handle. So we handled it anyway. We made a hotline. That's what you do, right? We didn't know! It just made sense to us, so that's what we did. How do you even make a hotline? We had to figure that out, too. 419-561-

5433. If you look at the last 4 numbers, 5433 spells "life" on a telephone keypad. Now THAT is a fucking lifeline.

The project grew so fast, it's unbelievable. Team Recovery had thousands of fans on Facebook. We had a hotline to manage. People wanted to give us money. We suddenly needed a board of directors. We needed help from lawyers, judges and attorneys, including ones that had sentenced us in the past. We needed an accountant. Politicians reached out to us and helped us get this thing moving. An attorney helped us by sending an application to the IRS to make us official.

We became a legit organization, with a board, with by-laws, and policies about conflicts of interest and whistleblowers. We developed a website. We didn't know a damn thing about how any of this worked when we started.

Keep in mind: *we are still in rehab at this point.*

We couldn't have done it without all these people who came to help us out. Well… maybe we could, but it would have taken a lot longer and been a hell of a lot more difficult. There's no way to express the gratitude I feel. All we did was hold up a sign. That's it. And so many people came to help. We were a group of people who were high on drugs, homeless, and thieving just a few *weeks* earlier. Complete strangers came from everywhere, believing in us and what we wanted to do. Toledo saw what was going on and knew something had to change.

Team Recovery was founded by people who robbed this community, and yet the community was still so generous to us. You helped us stay accountable. You helped us stay sober. We needed to give back.

***

I was running a business with babies, and I was a baby, too. I didn't know what a 501c3 was. I didn't know about zoning permits and what makes Facebook posts go viral. We all had to figure it out as we went. Along the way, tough decisions had to be made. People fell off. Some relapsed. New people wanted to join.

We didn't let just anyone sign up for our mission. We had a lot of interested parties. A lot. We didn't want everyone. We wanted only serious people, the not-here-to-play people, not-here-to-feel-good-about-myself people. Our name meant something to us. We took pride in it. We still do. Joining Team Recovery was a process more like joining the Navy Seals than attending a Sunday church potluck. You're not getting in unless you show us you have what it takes.

This is a team. You want to be on the team, there are tryouts. I played an exhibition game for scouts when I was in college. This is the same thing.

People who wanted to get involved were prospects, not members, just like a fraternity or a biker gang. There were rules. They weren't suggestions. If they messed up, they were out.

- 90 days sober, no exceptions.
- Submit to drug testing when asked, no exceptions.
- Prospects must attend a presentation with a member, no exceptions.
- Prospects must be there for any OD call. If you don't answer the phone, if you don't make it to the hospital, you're out. No exceptions.
- Prospects had to attend family support meetings and get a taste of everything we were doing. No exceptions.

After 3 months of that, our board of original members made the final decision.

Since 2015, only about 50 prospects have ever become members. Most prospects wash out. We didn't do it this way because we are hardasses or mean. It's for their sake, too.

When people get clean and begin their recovery, they often have a new, youthful exuberance. The "high on life" person. That newfound energy and enthusiasm doesn't always last. Not everyone can maintain that. That is why we tested people so hard. Many of our prospects were great people with lots of potential, but they weren't ready. They still needed to work on themselves. They hadn't mastered their own sobriety yet. Much of early recovery is finding a sponsor, going to meetings, getting a home group, and personal work. They need to get themselves right and not become distracted by throwing themselves into it before they can handle it. That's hard fucking work. Being an addict is a full-time job, *even while you're sober.* There are absolute units who work two full-time jobs (God bless them) but most who try will end up failing at both jobs.

We're not doing you any favors if you aren't ready. If and when you are, everything else we do can be taught. When you come to us, we are tough, but we're always rooting for you.

Chapter 29: In Court, This Time By Choice

Things I learned in recovery might seem trite or obvious. I hope they are. I sincerely hope you know all this stuff already and that all of this is boring the hell out of you because you are way ahead of the curve. Sometimes recovery feels like Kindergarten—especially in the beginning—because you don't even know what the right thing is.

I got sober at 27, but maturity-wise, I was still the same age as when I started drinking. I was still 16. No car, no license, no bank account. No idea of how to be an adult in any meaningful sense.

It's not obvious that you should turn yourself in for warrants. It's not obvious how to be a dad. It's not obvious that you should pay off the debt that you owe.

Doing the right thing takes practice. You need to do the right thing every day. You need to do the right thing twice a day just to get caught up.

I had to get started on all of that.

But my first priority was the person who should have been my first priority all along: my son.

***

At this point in the story, you probably don't trust me. You probably started this thing rooting for me. By now, you're probably waiting for me to fuck this up, too. That's good. It took some people years to get there. Maybe by the end of this book, I can win you back. I had to win a lot of people back. It's easier to trust someone you met a week ago than someone who's been lying and scamming for years. I don't deserve trust, and that's why trust is so precious to me now.

With Jackson's mom, just a microscopic amount of trust took about a year. We had no contact at all. I couldn't see my son. I couldn't speak to him on the phone. If I tried sending a gift, she'd say no. She didn't want me to get his hopes up and then leave again. As far as my son was concerned, I may as well be dead. Zero-contact.

While I was still actively addicted, she wanted me to sign away all rights to Jackson, with no right to negotiate and no right to dictate terms. I wasn't angry. Why should I be? She's the one who should be angry. She was just trying to do the best thing for our son. But I wasn't willing to lose him forever.

I didn't know anything about family law. I didn't even know where to start. I went to a buddy at the recovery house. He was napping, and I said, "Hey, man. I need to go to court to get my son back." In retrospect, I don't understand how he even heard me. He was dead asleep.

He instantly woke up and was on his feet, and he said, "Let's go."

He had a car. He didn't have plates. He was still using temporary tags that had expired two years ago, just a soggy piece of paper somehow holding on violating all laws of nature, not to mention other laws. He didn't have a driver's license. He didn't even have a stereo, because he'd sold that. He did have a Bluetooth speaker held onto the dash with a suction cup. We went downtown to a government building. I asked them what to do and I filled out the paperwork they told me to fill out.

That set into motion the process. Jackson's mom and I went back and forth in court 10 or 15 times. I didn't know the system when I started. I have a good sense of it now. I didn't have any plan except to never give up. I can get obsessed with things. I could be obsessed with this.

The work I was doing probably helped my case, but I had no money for attorneys. I relied on contacts I met through my service work, and I was introduced to an attorney who pointed me in the right direction. That attorney knew about my work and she wanted to help. She worked on my case pro bono, which is exactly what I could afford.[27]

The process wears people down. Court date after court date, and I think my ex finally saw that this was going to happen. I'd like to think that my tenacity helped her see that I was turning things around, but I don't know. Thankfully, when I finally got to see Jackson, she didn't demand visits with court-supervised staff. She thought it would confuse Jackson, and it would just be weird. We started out slow. A few hours at a time with Jackson while she was there to supervise. Then some time with just us guys. Eventually, he stayed overnight. Then two nights in a row. Finally, a shared parenting schedule.

It took a year just to get that first overnight. It was worth it.

---

[27] I made it up to her, though. Now she's my in-house counsel, and I thankfully am able to pay her. She's since helped represent me on cleaning up my felonies.

Chapter 30: Meet The Boss

I was invited out to a rally in Wooster, OH. That's Amish country. I spoke there, and told my story. It was a good crowd. A lot of them were that other type of drug abuse victim: people like my mom and my son. After these rallies, people approached me to thank me and share their stories with me. Everywhere I went, I met wounded people, collateral damage of the addiction in their community. Even in Amish country.

A couple of folks from Florida approached me after.

"You were great, man. We really admire what you're doing. I can see a lot of people are coming to you for help. We would love it if you could be a business development rep for us. You can direct some of those people our way, to our treatment center in Florida." These guys were smooth. They wanted me to be a salesman. I get attention. People come to me for help. Then I send them south to them.

I was basically like, "Fuck you." I don't know if those were my exact words, but my tone would have conveyed that message even if my words were more polite. "First, I don't know anything about you. Second, I know that south Florida is a shitshow with patient brokering and other unethical shit people are doing down there. No. I don't foresee that happening."

"I love that you said that." They didn't react the way I thought they would. "Here's what I'll offer you. Call my secretary. We'll book a flight for you. We'll bring you down and you can learn everything you want to know about us. I want you to know we're not like that. We're a good place."

That deflated my assumptions about them.

***

So I did it. I flew down there. I figured it was March. I'm in Ohio. The worst-case scenario is I get a day or two of good weather. I was just a few months into recovery. Routine, schedule, predictability, and stability are important, especially early on. Luckily, it's easy to find meetings in Florida.

When I got there, the place was not what I expected. I told you about pill mills. There are also recovery mills. The same medical system that got rich getting people hooked on pills was ready to make big money getting them *off* the pills. Those places treated people with the same pessimism as the COs I saw in jail: "Buh-bye. See you back here next week."

This place wasn't a recovery mill. It was… nice. A lot of places are nice, though. What mattered was these guys knew what they were doing.

They were 12-step based. They were abstinence-based. It wasn't just therapy and sitting in groups. It was wraparound services. It was way beyond anything we had in the midwest. If a patient had a court case (many of them do), they would get that patient to their county and attend the court date with them. They'd help people get driver's licenses and IDs so they could get a job when they got out. They were treating the whole person. They were helping them fix their whole lives.

As I was getting the grand tour, I said, "There is *nothing* like this in Ohio."

The place was great. I'd be happy to recommend it to anyone who asks. But still, why send people all the way to Florida? You don't get on a plane and fly 1300 miles for any other psychological problem. They hadn't convinced me to work for them. But they definitely inspired me. There's no reason Florida can have a place like this but we can't. We *need* this back home.

"I want you to meet the boss."

***

"Hey, what's up man! I'm Mike!" He said it like we were old college buddies who hadn't seen each other in a few years, bumping into each other at the grocery store. He was a short guy with relatively big ears, wearing a Star Wars t-shirt, jeans, and Adidas tennies.

The guy I met in the office was not what I expected. I thought he'd be like Mr. Burns from The Simpsons, a real titan-of-industry type. An older guy with white hair and an expensive Italian suit sitting behind a mahogany desk. I imagined he would cut a cigar with hands covered in gold rings, and while he puffed on it, he would check his Rolex often because he's a busy man and he wants me to know it.

The guy I met… honestly, for a second there, I thought maybe he was the guy who was going to introduce me to the *actual* boss.

"You want a cigar?" he offered. Well, I was right about the cigar, at least. His office wasn't anything like Don Giovanni's office in The Godfather. Mike had toys. Star Wars and horror movie action figures. My initial reaction was, *Mike's sort of a nerd.*

"No, I'm good, thanks."

We sat down and he gave the same pitch that his guys gave me in Wooster. "What do we have to do to get you sending people our way?"

It was a fair question. What was I even doing here? Just four months ago, I was a couple pounds of pressure away from eating a bullet from a stolen gun in my mom's garage. What *did* I want? There's a certain simplicity when you're using. You only want one thing. Now that I was four months clean, I couldn't lean on fentanyl to answer that question. It's crazy that I was even in that room with Mike. I had a dark history. I had felonies. I didn't exactly have the resumé of a model employee. For the first time in my life, I wasn't in a hurry to get out of rehab. This was an incredible opportunity. I was 4 months sober and this guy is trying to give me a job? A *good* job.

But it didn't feel right. I wanted to do this work, but not like this.

The baseball player in me came back at that moment. The mind game. When a pitcher and batter are facing off, it's a lot like the last two guys standing in a poker game. It's about feeling each other out. Trying to figure out what they'll do before they know what they'll do. Look for tells. Try to hide what you're up to. Two guys staring each other down, and the moment the ball is in the air, you just see how well they did. Bait them into swinging at an inside ball. Lay down a perfect bunt when they think you're swinging for the fences. I loved that about baseball.

"I don't think it's gonna work," I said.

"What can we do to make it work?"

"It doesn't make sense for me to send people from up in Ohio and Michigan down here. I'll do it, but I want a treatment center in Toledo. A good place, like you have here." I pushed all my chips in.

He stood up. "Thanks for coming down and having this meeting with me." He extended a hand to shake. The meeting was over, I guess. I shook it and I walked out of the office.

Mike had called my raise. Fuck. *Fuck*. I think I fucked it up. I asked for too much.

As I was leaving the facility, I asked my guide, "He just shook my hand and ended the meeting. Is that bad?"

He knew exactly what I meant, and said, "You just never know with him."

Mike was sort of nerdy, sure. He isn't intimidating when you meet him. But don't underestimate him. The man is sharp. If he had the arm for it, he'd be deadly on a pitcher's mound.

Chapter 31: Don't Celebrate In The First Half (It's Always The First Half)

As I planned, I had a free weekend in Florida. It didn't go the way I'd hoped, but it didn't matter. I didn't expect anything and that's what I got. Things back home were going well and I wasn't cutting corners.

It was really soon after I got back, I checked my voicemail messages. I pressed the button. "Hey, man! It's Mike! Gimme a call when you get the chance."

I called him back.

"Hi, Matt! I thought about your offer. So first thing, I need you to find a building. It needs to be zoned…" he gave the precise specs for a treatment center in Toledo, the size, the amenities, and listing off every bureaucratic obstacle and the thick jungle of red tape I'd have to machete through. I guess I got the job.

"Whoa, whoa, whoa. Slow down. Find a building? I don't know anything about zoning. What even is zoning?"

"You said you wanted a treatment center. You'll figure it out."

"Okay. I'll figure it out." I felt it was a challenge. Was this an early test? Was this the real interview? Did he need to see me prove I could figure it out? Don't ever threaten me with a good time. I'll learn zoning law better than a commercial real-estate attorney.

General George Patton supposedly said,

> *Don't tell people how to do things. Tell them what to do and let them surprise you with their results.*

I don't know if he really said that. There are lots of fake quotes on the internet, but damn… whoever did say that was on the money. Maybe it was Mike.

***

Team Recovery began as volunteer work. Team Recovery never stopped with that work, but my focus dramatically shifted towards opening a treatment center, Midwest Recovery Center. Mike brought the money. I brought the knowledge of addiction, recovery, and Toledo. Mike was like a genie making a wish come true… but I had to work. And I did. I had to learn so much as I went, maybe I'll write a whole book just about how to start a place because it's that involved. Licensing, permits, and inspections by a dozen different agencies, and half of them sound like they do the same job. I had to figure it all out as I went. It wasn't a chore. This was a gift. A challenge. Something to fight for every day. Something to give to the people of Toledo; exactly what I needed when I was using. I'd taken so much. I'd robbed, scammed, hustled, leeched, and bullshitted this community for years. I wasn't going to let anything stop me from repaying what they were owed.

Finding a building isn't just about finding a building. You can't just open up a treatment center. I went to the city council and put my name on the line, promising that this would be a benefit to the community. Believe it or not, people usually aren't thrilled to learn there's about to be a building full of addicts down the block. I can promise you, it doesn't do any favors for your property value. I had to get a special use permit. I had to go to the council meetings and organize the town halls. I had to convince the community that this was going to be done right, that we were good people who were going to make this place better. That's not easy, especially when anyone can see the quality of some of these detoxes, and the prostitutes and dealers creeping around them like sharks smelling blood. It's not easy to prove your place will be different when so many other places made the same promises and failed.

We did it. Somehow we did it.

I didn't buy into Midwest Recovery, but I was offered sweat equity through work. After 365 days into this project, I became a minority owner by building this place from nothing. If I quit working, I still owned my piece. Even if I relapsed and went back to the streets, I still owned a part of it.

I loved it. I was happy. We started with 22 beds. I couldn't remember ever being this happy before. Midwest Recovery Center remains one of the biggest treatment centers in Ohio, with almost 500 beds in Toledo, Youngstown, and soon, Cincinnati. I spent a year making that happen and I had no idea how.

***

These things aren't cheap. Mike didn't pay out of pocket. He had to bring in some other investors. They didn't know anything about drugs and alcohol, but they knew the business. These were investors, not donors. They expected growth, and returns, they expected to see their money make more money, like any investor.

When they got in, I had no say. This happened before my first year, before I had any ownership. And things changed. The money helped. We grew so fast. I was making them tons of money. It grew *too* fast.

It wasn't the small, hometown thing I imagined. It wasn't what it started as. It slowly became exactly like every other treatment center. It became another copy of the same model that wasn't working. It wasn't bad. Some places are bad, and this was not one of them. But it wasn't what I was trying to do.

They cut spending. Cut staffing. Lowered the quality of food.

I wanted people to have real food, another part of the physical recovery after detoxing. I wanted it well-staffed so employees were fresh and happy to come to work, not burned out, overworked, and underappreciated. I wanted it to be *fun*.

This isn't it. I fought it the whole way.

This was my baby. I was the co-founder and CEO. It was my connections, my work that made it all happen. But it wasn't my money, and in the end, that's what counts.

"You can't do this to my center." I told them.

"Don't ever say that again. This is not your center. Let me make it very clear. You are a minority owner. Don't get things twisted."

The way they saw it, cutting one nurse was $50k right in their pocket. It made no sense to me. They're already making millions, so what's it to them to hire just one more nurse? Every penny mattered to them.

They weren't interested in trying something new. They weren't interested in our experiment in what treatment can be. They understood the formula. They knew the safe system. They weren't interested in taking chances on something no one had done before. They wanted easy, reliable money.

There are plenty of grocery store chains. Why start a new one if you're just going to copy someone else's formula and try to compete with them? This place was supposed to be different. If it's exactly like every other place, what's the point of going with us instead of anywhere else? What makes it special? They knew accounting. They ran nursing homes and had vast real-estate portfolios. They knew how to make money doing that stuff. The enterprise I was trying to make didn't work that way. They didn't get it. I did.

We clashed so much, they got sick of the headache. They finally made me an offer I couldn't refuse. Literally.

"Take it or leave it. If you stay, you won't work here anymore, but we will *increase* your salary. You don't have to report to the office anymore. In fact, you don't have an office anymore. No one reports to you. You have no operational control at all. Or you can leave."

I didn't know what to do. For the first time, I didn't have any clear path. I carried Midwest Recovery to term, and it was taken just like that. When I got the keys to the building and walked into it for the first time, I looked around at the blank, half-painted drywall, it was just an empty space with a roof. I personally demoed walls with a sledgehammer.

But more than just the building, this was my project. This was what I was about now. This experiment in better treatment was who I was. It's what I did. It's how people knew me. It's how I knew myself. It represented the clean me, the one who didn't even hear my phone vibrate anymore when my crazy ex-girlfriend Heroin started texting. Shit. This was *my* recovery center for *me*. Running this place played a part in motivating *me* to stay sober. What the hell was I supposed to do without it?

That was hard. Watching helplessly as the thing you invested your heart and soul into becomes a hollowed-out version of itself is devastating. It was like my baby, and it was like watching my child become addicted to drugs. Watching your child sell their soul. Maybe I was getting a little taste of what I'd fed my mother for all those years.

At the start of this book, at the start of my story, I told you that drugs started as a way of getting control. The two times I felt most powerless in my life were when I lost Midwest Recovery and when I lost my father. Weakness scares me. I was vulnerable for so many years.

God answers all prayers. Sometimes the answer is, "No."

Chapter 32: Don't Think You Got This

It threw me, man. I wasn't myself. I was a dick. I was unpleasant to be around. Frankly, I was miserable and angry all the time.

The things that are needed the most are the things you won't get paid for. Treatment is lucrative, but there's no money in prevention. You can't make a living going to schools and telling kids how not to throw it all away or visiting people who have overdosed in the hospital. The program needed the money, but the money came with strings that corrupted it. It was a catch-22. You can't have the treatment if you don't have the money, but you can't get the money without ruining it.

If my dad was still around, he would be the guy I'd want to talk to. But the next best person for the job is my mentor. He's a man who's been sober for about 13 years. He's very successful and very good with money. Like so many recovering addicts, whatever that energy is that drives you to chase the object of addiction, it doesn't go away when you get sober. It's channeled elsewhere. He channeled it into creativity and growth. He's polished but not flashy. Classy. He still goes to his home group. He still sponsors people. He still does the work.

He was the man to ask.

***

I'm going to say something that might sound radical. I believe that sober addicts are one of America's most undervalued resources. I truly mean that. When you pass by an addict on the street—when you try to avoid eye contact with a disheveled person who tells you a sad lie about their broken-down car and how they need money for a cab—you might be walking past an entrepreneur who was ruined by drugs. Seriously. You are avoiding a person who should be a small business owner, a salesperson with the best sales record in the company, or a person who shows up early and leaves work late. That person can and should be addicted to a *mission*, not a chemical.

I said that addiction isn't a hobby, it's a vocation. Doctors passed out countless millions of very addictive pills. Most people who had dental surgery in 2007 didn't end up on the streets selling their bodies for dope money. The addict's brain is different. A person with that same singular, laser focus can direct it towards doing good instead of using it to slowly murder themselves.

When you show a tennis ball to a dog, they stop. They freeze. Their eyes are on the ball. Not one muscle moves. There is only that ball. There is only the anticipation for what comes next. And when you throw the ball, the dog takes off so fast that their first few bounds just slide on the floor like a cartoon. They fly at the ball like a heat-seeking missile. There is nothing else in the world that they would rather do than go get that ball and bring it back to you. Once they have it, their tail wags so hard you can hear it slapping back and forth. They rush back because they cannot wait to give it back and do it again. Addicts are like this. The tennis ball can be crack cocaine, alcohol, gambling, or sex. But it can also be athletics, community, art, or business. Addiction is, I believe, fundamentally a double-edged sword. Whatever that tennis ball drive is, it can be used for good or evil.

***

So, I asked my mentor—I don't even know what I asked, the question didn't even matter—I just needed someone to help me figure this out. And like a wise monk in a Tibetan monastery, he answered my question with a question.

"Matt, lemme ask you this. If you were working a job making eight bucks an hour and you didn't like the way the owners were doing things, what would you do? I know what you would do, but I want to hear you say it."

"I would quit. If they're doing something that's not okay, then I don't want to be a part of it."

"You're making a lot more than eight bucks an hour doing this. But you haven't resigned. So why is that the case?"

"Because I'm making good money. I have a real livelihood. A career." It felt weird to say that out loud, like I was just realizing it for the first time.

"As a person in recovery, is the money worth more than your values? Is it worth more than your morals?"

Shit. He made me say it. He made me say it out loud because I needed to hear myself say it. And it clicked. That was the true intention of their bargain. They offered to pay me more to buy my compliance. They offered me a beautiful, diamond-studded prison cell. And I almost took that bargain. It was the practical thing to do. It seemed crazy to turn it down.

My mentor was right. Mentors usually are. They weren't just taking away my program. They were taking away the thing that was part of my new identity as sober Matt. They wanted me in shiny, golden handcuffs.

Fuck 'em. They can keep their money. I did it before. I can do it again. And it'll be easier this time because this time I already know I can, and I already know how. Goodbye, Midwest Recovery. Back to Team Recovery.

It's no secret that Hollywood is full of very wealthy, very unhappy people and that Hollywood also has its share of drug abusers. That old cliché, "Money can't buy you happiness," always seemed quaint. It turns out it's true. I had money. I wasn't happy.

I sold my equity for pennies on the dollar.

Chapter 33: The Devil Never Goes Away

People in Florida know to put up the shutters before the hurricane gets there. Some problems will make themselves known long before they find you. Plan ahead.

It's not a matter of if. It's a matter of when, and how bad. There will be a hurricane. Be ready for it or be ruined by it.

When I was high, I was only thinking ahead to the next high. Sober Matt was looking ahead by *years*.

It was a year before I made a dollar at Team Recovery, and even when it opened and we started receiving payments for the services we were providing, I didn't put myself on salary for the first 9 months. It was two years before I was paid. Be frugal like Dad was. That was only possible because I was ready to make it possible. I could live off what I had saved from Midwest Recovery for as long as it took to build what Toledo needed. I had it all planned out. I had all my ducks in a row.

***

Some people stay as far from substances as they can. I get that. I know a man who won't eat BBQ sauce if Jack Daniel's name is on the label. He knows it won't get him drunk, but that's not the point. The point is he won't move one inch, not even one nanometer away from sobriety. Once you start giving yourself allowances, it's easy to give yourself another and another, until you're telling yourself all the reasons why the needle in your arm won't be like last time. I understand that. Especially for people who are just out of detox and back in the world with the Earth-people.

If you drink a beer in front of me, for a couple seconds, I'll think to myself, "Damn. That looks kind of good." I'll think about the good times at Bier Stube. The first drink I had in high school, and making out with girls.

It took me a long time to understand that those thoughts will always be there. Recovery isn't about never having those thoughts again. It's about training myself to remember the second half of the story. The first part is the fun part, the parties, the laughing, the friends. Those thoughts come easily and on their own. I believed that if I couldn't get rid of those thoughts, I couldn't be sober.

That's addict mentality. That's an excuse. Addict logic doesn't care what the question is, the answer is always the same, and it's *always* the wrong answer.

You see some ice cream at the grocery store. Do you buy it and eat the whole thing in your car in the parking lot? You see someone on Facebook is selling a pristine teal 1954 Cadillac El Dorado. Do you drop $80k on it? Just because a good-looking woman tries flirting with you, do you cheat on your wife? Temptation never goes away.

The first time anyone threw me a baseball, I didn't catch it. I was a kid. I barely knew how to use my arms. But after years and years of training, I could catch a ball moving faster than the cars on your daily work commute. I don't have to think about it anymore. I don't have time to think. I only have time to move. I'm already looking for where the ball needs to go the moment it's in my glove. A general manager can't do everything. They have to delegate responsibility to other people who are well-trained and experienced, people they trust can do the job. In sports, the body is like that. I have to trust my arms and legs to do the job, because I'm thinking about the big picture, about what happens next.

Sports are also about training the mind. Blocking out distractions. Thinking so fast, you don't even hear your own mind, you just watch yourself do it. That's why I can watch you drink a beer and not order one for myself. As soon as I remember the good times, I remind myself of the bad times. I don't have to try. Not anymore. I've trained myself. I still hear that voice trying to hustle me, trying to con me, to bullshit me. It tries to bullshit me just like that addict on the sidewalk tries to bullshit you when you walk by. It tells a story that isn't true or is only half true. I tell that bullshitter inside me the other half of the story. I tell that bullshitter the part that came after the fun part. The bad times. The worst times. The worst times for me, but also the worst times for Mom. The worst times for Jackson. Those are times I can't let Jackson's sisters ever see for themselves.

So I look at that beer. It looks good. There are beads of condensation accumulating on the tall glass, like in a TV commercial. Golden yellow, like the tall grains of American wheat in a political ad. Yeah. It looks good. But not as good as my wife. Not as good as my kids. Not as good as my mom. My house. My weekends. My life.

If you're in recovery now, reading this book, or listening to it on audio, I want you to hear this loud and clear. It's what I wish someone had told me when I was where you are right now.

The devil in you never goes away and never gets weaker. So you need to get stronger.

***

One thing that separates baseball from other popular American sports is that baseball doesn't have a game clock. It doesn't matter how far ahead you are or how behind you are. This inning is the most important. This is the inning that can win the game or cost the game. You can't take an early lead and run out the clock. As Yogi Berra said, "It ain't over til it's over." In a three-game series, it ain't even over when it *is* over.

That was the attitude I needed. Sobriety isn't something you finish. It's never over. My work was never over, either. This time, no investors. No partners. I'm doing it on my own. I used the money I'd saved up and put it to work. I invested in myself.

Midwest Recovery wasn't a bad treatment center. I don't want to give the impression that they were bad. They weren't a recovery mill that cashed checks and churned people in and out like a county jail. The problem was they weren't good enough. They weren't what they *could* be.

I had friends. I had contacts. I had knowledge about the processes, the bureaucracy, and the system. I got a building. I got some apartments. I got the necessary licenses, quietly. I got accredited. State license. Medicaid license.

I started small. I would have to build. I could have been discouraged and frustrated. I *was*. One thing I am eternally grateful to Midwest Recovery for is that they showed me that I could do it. I wasn't hoping I could. I was doing it again. *This* is my tennis ball. Throw it again and I'll chase it again. I love this ball and I will chase it all damn day.

Chapter 34: How?

My last time in therapy, a therapist asked me, "You've been an athlete. You've been a father. You've been all these things. Have you ever once been a man of character?"

There's no sting quite like a question you don't want to answer. "No. I haven't. How do I even do that?"

She was really good. She was the one who finally made me face that my father's passing hit me harder than I would admit. Harder than I was ready for. *Matt isn't fine.*

Why did it work? It was everything together. Therapy + positive support group + Team Recovery folks + AA meetings + my sponsor + God + service work… you can't make a cookie and leave out one or two ingredients, or you'll end up with butter, eggs, and sugar.

When you get clean, everything has to change. The people you hang with, the way you think, the way you talk… that person has been fucking up nonstop for too long. You have to be someone who's better than the person you used to be.

I finally understood that I'm *not* different. I'm *not* the exception. Thank God that I'm not, because that means that everything that worked for me is something I could share.

She was the one to finally get it to click for me.

That's why I hired her at Team Recovery.

I didn't know it at the time, but while I was learning to unfuck myself, I was also scouting for talent. The people I hired at Team Recovery are the best people I met while I was getting treated. I went back and found a lot of the good folks in this book to build my dream team, my best of the best. If treatment were a competition in the Olympics, I would bring the same people that I work with every day. Not only did I see my people do their job, I experienced it firsthand. No resumé or degree can compete with that.

We are not about putting people into a room and billing insurance. I'm not interested in repeat business. I'm interested in the humans that walk through our door. I know their mom. I know the judge who sent them to me. Their probation officer who recommended me. This is a community and I have a responsibility to it now.

The businessmen, the bean-counters couldn't understand that the business was built on relationships. It's about earning people's trust in a world where trust is more rare than a Mickey Mantle rookie card. It's about doing a good job so they tell the next person that there is *one* place to go. Reputations are fragile. If you tell 10 truths and a lie, you're a liar. Trust is earned and that's why I only want the best.

I hope I'm not sounding like an advertisement right now. I just really love my job and I'm so proud of the people I work with and the reputation we've built. I almost wrote that I get to save lives, but that's not exactly true. What I get to do is actually better than that. I help people save themselves.

I do want to say just one last thing about Team Recovery, though. Remember back on that street where I had the worst date night of all time? The one where I overdosed and Monica saved me. After doing this work for years, we now have 14 buildings on that street, all sober living houses. I nearly died on that street, and right now, there are about 90 people in recovery in those houses.

It doesn't feel real sometimes.

***

People came back. It just sort of happened on its own. People I loved and missed started coming back. When I stopped chasing them, they just came back to me. It's strange. Long after I stopped trying to reach her, Mom finally called. She wanted to take me out for lunch. She offered to bring me groceries. She always brought me socks. To this day, even at Christmas, she needs to know that I have enough socks. Just a mom thing.

I was sober in a way I never was before. I'd been clean before but drugs were always in my mind. For the first time since high school, I wasn't thinking about getting high.

I stopped chasing people, and my friends and family came back to me. Free was my gateway to get paid. Giving away paid me back. It's wild to think about. I missed them so much and the way to get them back was to just leave them the hell alone. The only way to prove that I wouldn't use them, lean on them, betray them, was to just leave them the hell alone.

I got my mom back. I got my son back. I got Monica back. I even married her, just like I told my tattoo artist I was going to do.

Monica's parents were cautious of me. Rightfully so. It took years to earn their trust. Now we're family.

Even my own mom will drug test me. I'm serious! Anytime she wants a cup of her son's clean, drug-free urine, I will gladly provide a sample. Maybe that sounds weird, I don't know. I owe it to her, though. She trusted me in a way only a mom can, and I somehow managed to wreck even that. So yeah. If she needs me to piss clean, I will do it with a smile on my face.

I'm a godfather to two kids. There was a time when people wouldn't even trust me with my own kid. Now they trust me with *theirs*. What an honor.

It has taken so long to get right. Getting married, getting back to church, getting caught up on child support. Getting right with the law, turning myself in to the police in Pittsburgh, Pennsylvania, completely sober. Turning myself in to Michigan for the home invasion warrant. I was high all those years, and it's taken me nearly as long to get back to baseline.

I have no warrants now. No criminal legal issues at all. When I started writing this book, I had filed for all of my felonies to be expunged. By the time I was finished and ready to publish, I was successful in those expungements. That blows my mind! Imagine me as a non-felon!

***

I love golfing now. I didn't think I would, but I really do. Monica's dad got me into it, and it's become a regular thing we do. We were playing at a course close to where Monica grew up—me, Pat, and Jackson—and I sliced a drive into someone's backyard.[28] The lady of the manor came out to greet us as we came to retrieve my ball. She was drunk as shit, and she struck up a conversation and told us all about her divorce. They split because he's an alcoholic in recovery and she's an alcoholic who refuses to get clean. It's amazing what people will tell you when they're loaded. The point of her story was that she was selling her house, and she doesn't care what she sells it for, because her husband's lawyer isn't very good and she gets half the listing price no matter what it sells for.

She saw Jackson and said to me, "I want your son to grow up in this house."

"Uh… it's a great place and all, but I can't afford this house."

"Just make an offer. I want your son to grow up in this house."

---

[28] I'm still working on that.

Here's what's crazy, though. I *just* got done paying off my car. I *just* got done paying off my student loans. I *just* got my credit in order and my debt-to-income ratio was good enough that I was there. I actually *could* get that house with her crazy 50% off discount. I wondered if maybe she was going to sober up and change her mind. She didn't. Her ex was very comfortable and she didn't mind wasting some of his money.

We bought that house for half of what it was worth. As an investment, we made money just by moving into it. We live there now. I live on a golf course now. *Me*. The guy who had his sheets and pillows stolen off his stack-a-bunk by hood rats on the 4th floor. The guy who slept in the busted down car behind his mom's house.

It's spooky. If I hadn't fixed all my money problems, if I hadn't messed up my swing in exactly the way I did to land in that woman's yard, if my son wasn't there... How? How does that happen? I think about all the things that had to come together just right at the right moment for me to survive that overdose with Monica, how if one thing was a little different, I'd be dead. Well, it happened again. And just to make it a little weirder, my wife grew up on the opposite side of *that same golf course*. My father-in-law was there to witness this, the first steps of me moving our family into the house just across the way from where he raised his. Three generations of us boys together that day.

I believe in coincidences, but damn. That one is hard to believe in.

***

I still go to schools to talk to kids. One time, a kid asked me a good question: "If you could go back and change anything, what would you do?"

My first thought was to say, "I wish I'd never smoked that first cigarette and never gone down that path." That was the easy thing to say. It was the obvious thing to say. I was there to tell kids not to do drugs, wasn't I? But it wasn't the truth. Adults lie to kids every day. They lie because they think that's what kids need to hear. Take it from a man who has told a lot of lies: when kids learn how much they were told wasn't true, it's not easy to earn it back. It's rare that kids hear adults talk to them straight, especially about tough subjects. When it happens, kids notice. They pay attention.

"No. I believe all this happened for a reason. I believe that God won't take you to something if you can't find your way through something."

It's weird to think about now, but if I hadn't been on cocaine at that bar, at that time, on that night, I wouldn't have seen the best woman I've ever met. That can't be an accident.

That's what I believe and that's what I told them. If I had a time machine, I wouldn't go back, find my younger, dumber self, and slap a needle out of his arm. If things hadn't gone the way they had, there wouldn't be a Jackson, Gigi, or Giuliana in my life. There wouldn't be Monica. I wouldn't be doing what I'm doing right now. Do you think I could trade all this for baseball? I love baseball. I *love* it. But there is no universe where I would trade what I have now for that.

When I was in the third chapter of my life (the third chapter of this book), I thought that was it. That was the story. Good stories don't work that way. Name a good sports movie where the main character gets a scholarship, goes to college, plays for the MLB for 15 years, retires a hero, and that's that. That's like a Disney movie where the princess hooks up with the prince in the first scene and they live happily ever after for the next 90 minutes. The end, roll credits.

That's not a good story, because it's not real life. It's boring. Real life has problems, conflicts, challenges, failures, and victories.

The Bad News Bears don't start out loving each other and using teamwork.

Now I'm literally writing the book of my life and the last chapter in it won't be the last chapter, because I still have so much shit to do.

Chapter 35: Step 9

Step 9 is making amends. For me, that was the hardest. Accepting responsibility. Cleaning up your messes. Confronting the people you hurt, knowing some of them will never forgive you. I burned a lot of bridges. I hurt a lot of people. It is ego-destroying having to face your mess and clean it up. Destroying my ego was the best thing for me.

When you're sober, you can't hide from your own guilt. It will eat at you. If you don't deal with it, it often drives you to relapse.

I'm a Catholic boy. We have a tradition of confessing and admitting to ourselves and to God what we did wrong. We can't be forgiven until we confess. I'll tell you though, it is so much easier to say sorry to God than it is to the person you hurt. I've had a lot to confess to God but I never had to look Him in the eyes when I did it. I never felt God pour shame into me the way people will. God forgives. People usually don't let you off so easily. They will use the opportunity to read you a full accounting of everything you ever did wrong. The list is always longer than you thought it was. The damage you did was always deeper than you realized. It's brutal.

In a way, asking people for forgiveness isn't that different from what I'd been doing for years: asking the people I care about for something that I don't deserve. A lot of things come naturally to me. Not this. I don't think confronting the people you hurt comes naturally to anyone.

Even though things are extremely civil today and we have a strong co-parenting relationship, I don't think Jackson's mom will ever fully forgive me. Not all the way. I get it. I fucked her life up. A lot of people won't forgive. That's okay. I lost the right to negotiate how things are going to go. She loves Monica, though.

If you cheat on your wife, and you work it out, you don't get to be mad when she brings it up again. It doesn't matter if she says she forgives you. You don't get to demand that she forgets it happened, and remind her that she forgave you. She forgives you or she doesn't. She feels how she feels about it. It's not up to the cheater to make demands on the terms of the relationship. And you look stupid as hell trying to.

I've worked so hard to pay off these spiritual debts and I fixed a lot, but I couldn't fix everything.

The fix that I needed most was for my mom. More than anyone, I had to fix what I did to her. I saved everything I could, and I paid off all that debt she took on from me as soon as I could. I bought her house and I moved her out of that neighborhood and way out into the country where she always wanted to be. That was the one debt that meant the most for me. Of all the debts on my conscience, hers was the heaviest.

***

I was at Home Depot and I bumped into an old friend. Not really a friend. More like an acquaintance. An acquaintance that I was very afraid of. Do you remember way back in chapter 13, when I mentioned the main plug in town? The guy who was sourcing directly from Mexican cartels? I saw him there. The former drug kingpin of Toledo, pushing an orange cart like a regular guy. He was out of federal prison, obviously. Was he there to get a circular saw to cut up bodies or something? Maybe he was building out another underground drug lair.

I saw him. He saw me. I wasn't sure if he recognized me. I kinda hoped he didn't. We went our separate ways, but he came back and found me.

"Hey, man."

Ah, shit. He did recognize me. "Hey."

I'll admit. I was nervous to talk to him. I might have been the last dude he showed that stash to in his house. For all I know, maybe he thinks I said something to the police.

"I just want to let you know. I'm happy for you." I guess he already knew what I'd been up to. "You were doing your thing back then. So was I. You changed. So have I. I had my consequences. I had to go away for a little bit. But I'm back and I'm not doing any of that shit again."

I remember back when he was not a man to be fucked with, a man with an arsenal in his basement that looked like where John Wick goes shopping. But he had changed. He was working construction and shopping at Home Depot for the job.

There are so many others I want to bump into at Home Depot, in the diaper aisle at Target, by the gazebo at the Old West End Festival, or anywhere else. I'd be happy with just the glance, the nod. A lot of us didn't get out alive. So many I lost count. I see them. They're healthy, happy, alive. They see me, and I'm the same way. We don't have to talk. In a way, you and me, the people we are now, we never really met. We don't have to relive anything or hash out old times. But I want you to know, whoever you are, I saw you, I recognized you, and I'm so damn glad to see you.

Chapter 36: The Guy In The Stands

People talk about getting high on life. It's corny, but I know what they mean. There are moments that are transcendental. They take you to a level you didn't know you could go. It's kind of like being high. Getting high will put you outside of the ordinary human experience, no matter what the drug is. It's all just dopamine, right?

Wrong.

There is a fundamental difference between snorting oxy and getting an eagle with my son on the 5th hole of Sylvania Country Club. That second kind of experience accumulates during your life. You nurture those moments and you collect them, like photographs on your mantle. Since I've been sober, I just keep finding those moments. I will never forget that brief moment on the hole with the highest handicap on the front 9 of that course. Jackson won't either. It's a kind of happiness in the bank of my life that collects interest and becomes more precious over time.

I still feel like I'm not supposed to be here. I'm in a golf cart with my son. My driver's license was suspended indefinitely. I didn't even know that was a thing until it happened to me. Now I own several cars. I slept in a garage. That was not easy to fix, but it was fixable. Now I own a beautiful house. I couldn't be trusted with my son, but I got my son back after everything I put him and his mom through, and two more kids who have tripled the love in my life.

I shouldn't even be here. I should be dead or in prison. How am I even *allowed* on a golf course?

What's great about golf is, it's just you vs. you. There are no excuses. You do it or you don't.

I can get addicted to anything. It could be alcohol, weed, crack, or fentanyl. What is the common denominator? What do all of those substances have in common? If you said, dopamine, that's a good guess, but it's not the right answer. The thing that all of those substances have in common is me. No one can put a needle in my arm but me.

People ruin their lives every day without drugs or alcohol. They commit crimes, go to jail, ruin marriages, and get fired from jobs.

"Through our inability to accept personal responsibility, we were actually creating our own problems." That was me back when I was blaming God. The unhappiest people in the world are the people who don't get how they contribute to their own unhappiness.

It's not about changing drugs. It's about changing who we are. If you take booze away from a drunk man who beats up his girlfriend, you don't make the abuser disappear. You just create a sober guy who beats up his girlfriend.

***

When I wake up, the very first thing I do is say the Third Step Prayer.

> *God, I offer myself to Thee — to build with me and to do with me as Thou wilt. Relieve me of the bondage of self, that I may better do Thy will. Take away my difficulties, that victory over them may bear witness to those I would help of Thy Power, Thy Love, and Thy Way of life. May I do Thy will always!*

Every night, I meditate. When I lay down to sleep, I think about my first home run. I fall asleep to that every night.

You know I love baseball. As soon as I knew what a home run was, I wanted to hit one. I trained my butt off for it. And when it finally happened, my dad was there to see it. That was everything to me. The person I wanted most in the world to impress, to be proud of me. That is a rare, and perfect moment. One of the happiest memories of my life. I remember every detail. It was a night game. The big lights illuminating the field, and the flying bugs swarming around them. The people on the aluminum stands, calling out their kids' names. I remember the smell of the summer, the fresh-cut grass in the humid air. I even remember the direction the wind was blowing. I remember taking my stance at the plate, conscientious to hold my bat right. I remember the pitch. I swung but didn't even feel the ball. That's what a perfect hit feels like. It feels like nothing. Just aluminum cutting through the air. I've hit countless home runs, but that's the only one I have a perfect mental record of. I remember the ritual of casually running the bases, passing by the other team's players who looked anywhere but at me. I remember my dad in the stands on the other side of the safety fence, smiling at me, clapping for me, calling me "champ."

After my dad was gone… who was I supposed to hit a home run for now? Who was my guy in the stands? Who was there for me every game?

When I was playing as a kid, the stands were just family. It was small. It was personal. Playing college ball on the field, looking up at the stands, the faces in the crowd are like leaves on a tree. You don't see each one, you just see the mass of color and movement.

A sponsor once asked me, "If drugs are your answer, what the fuck is your question?" It took me a long time and a lot of digging to find what that question was.

What is it about me that I dislike about myself that I feel like I can't have a relationship with the world? Why can't I dance sober at a wedding? Why isn't Matt good enough without the substance?

I like people. I wanted people to like me. I wanted their approval. But my all-time biggest fan—who would always be that person for me— the only person I really wanted to be that person for me… was my dad. I couldn't look in the stands and see his face there anymore. I'd see hundreds of faces where Roy's should've been. Faces of strangers. Leaves on a tree. If everyone in that crowd booed at me while my dad cheered me on, I would still call that a good day.

When I got that eagle in our backyard, Jackson and I had that same moment that my father and I had when I hit my first home run. I was able to give Jackson an experience that will be a perfect memory, just like the one I go to sleep thinking about every night. That memory is just ours. From now on, when my kids hit home runs, I get to be *their* guy in the stands.

Epilogue

My family is building a house. No. Let me rephrase that. My family is building a home. Since I started working on this book, we have added another member to the family. Giuliana is a year old now and being her father is the most amazing thing in the world.

Team Recovery is expanding significantly. Our formula is very simple, yet very few businesses have the courage to copy our model. We are the best because we hire the best. I hate to see talent working someplace that doesn't know what they can do, that doesn't let them do what they can do. Those are the people we want at Team Recovery. One of the joys of my job every day is working with amazing people and letting them impress the hell out of me.

I'm almost done with my bachelors degree! It's a dream I gave up on the day I lied to my coach and told him I didn't love baseball. But I'm doing it for real. When I graduate in the spring of 2024, I'll be a Licensed Social Worker. I currently have a 3.96 GPA and I'm graduating Summa Cum Laude (with the highest distinction). Oh yeah… I recently found out I got accepted into the Masters program at the same University that I dropped out of nearly 20 years ago due to my addiction.

I'm the elected chair for the board of directors of the OneOhio Foundation. This is the state foundation that received the settlement money from Purdue Pharma. You may remember those guys from way back in chapter 4, the company that made crazy money by aggressively pushing oxys. I have to say it feels damn good to take money from the company that did so much damage to me, my family, and millions of other Americans, and be given the great honor of using it for good. There's a lot of injustice in the world. It's nice to win once in a while.

We're at the end of this book, which means I'm on to the next thing. I have a lot more coming. I have a few more books planned. I'm working on a documentary about addiction. Lots of cool stuff, some of which I can't talk about just yet.

It's hard to take a day off when I love what I do this much.

***

I gave special thanks to a lot of people at the beginning of this book. If I named everyone who helped me, this would be a book of nothing but names. I hope no one takes offense if I didn't mention you. I promise you, my memory and my heart are longer than 60,000 words. So many people took a chance on me. They invested with me, they gave their time and money to me. More than that, they gave their name and risked their own reputations by vouching for me.

I love that I get to take chances on others like the way you all took a chance on me.

Like they said to me in that meeting all those years ago, *you can't keep it if you don't give it away.*

It's a lot of pressure on me to not fuck it up.

It's good, though. It helps me stay focused.

You all help me stay sober so that I get to live this wonderful life.